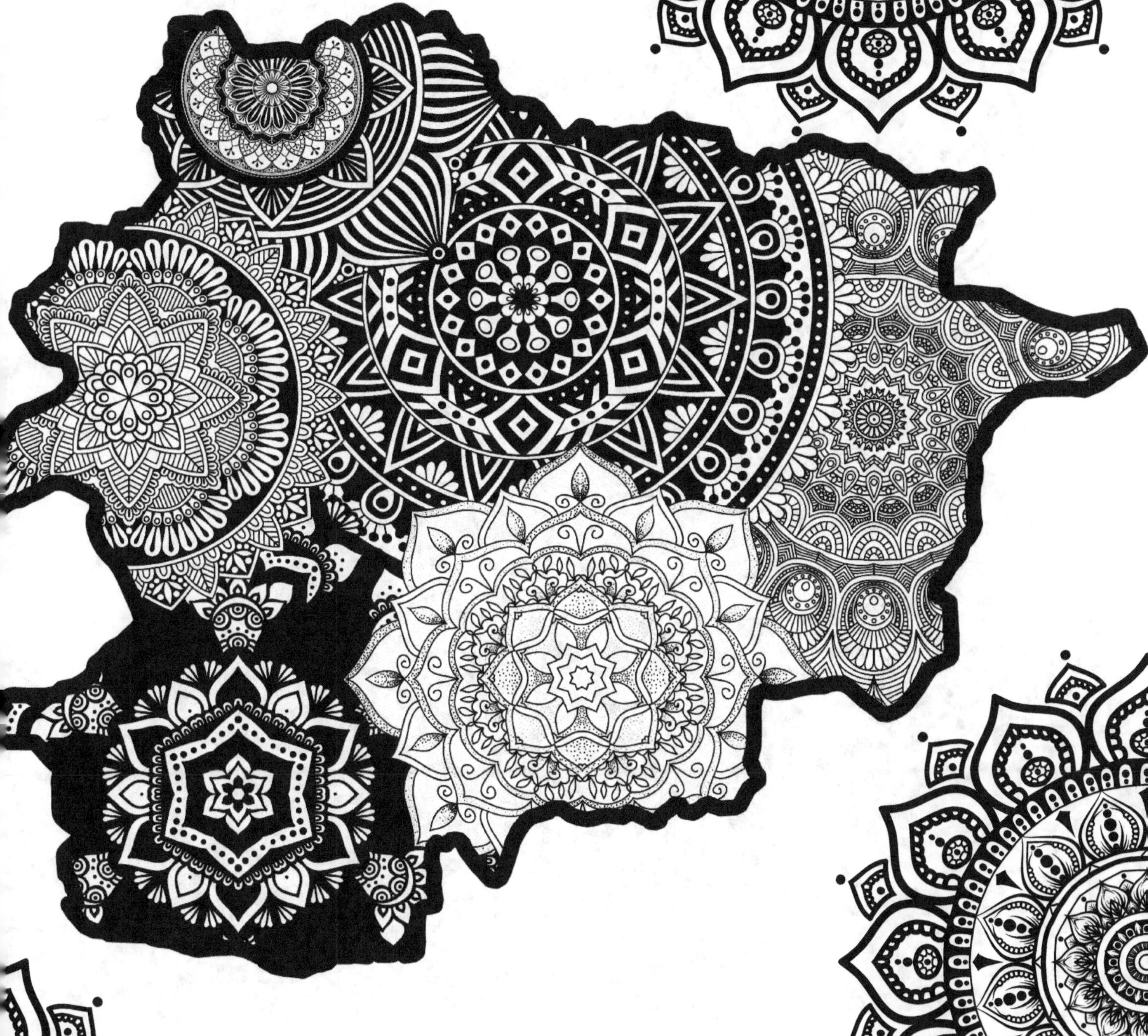

ANDORRA

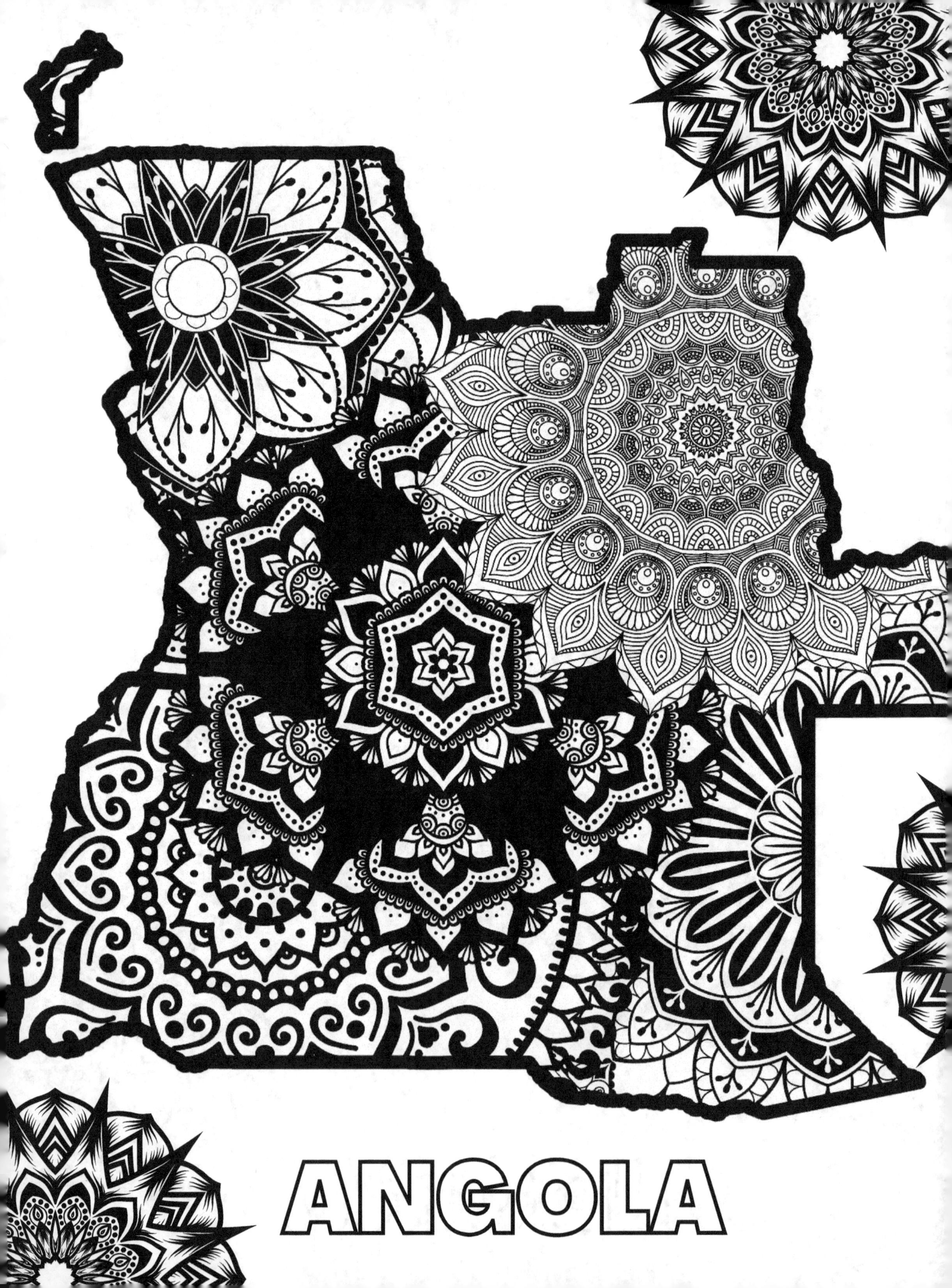

ANGOLA

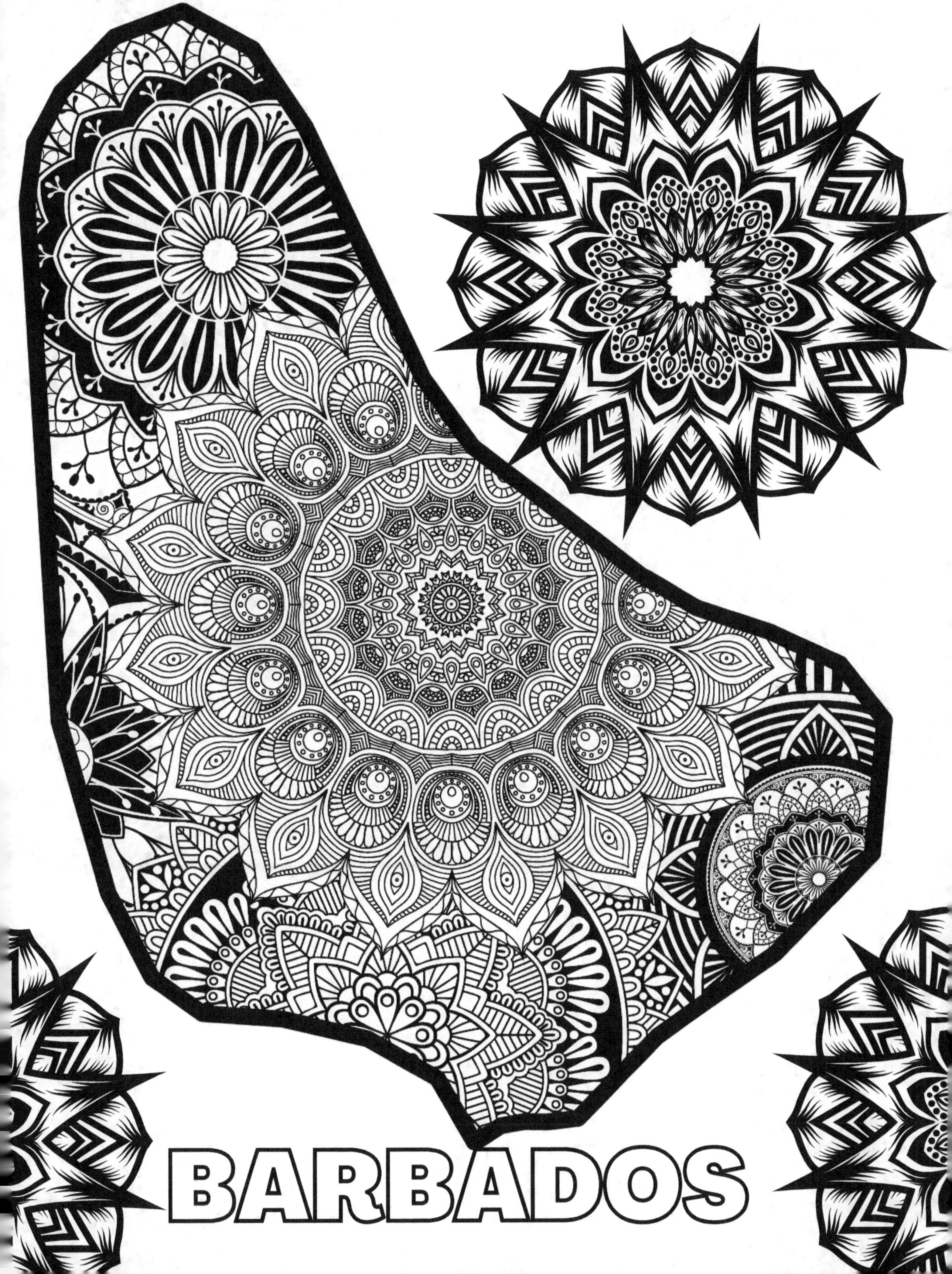
BARBADOS

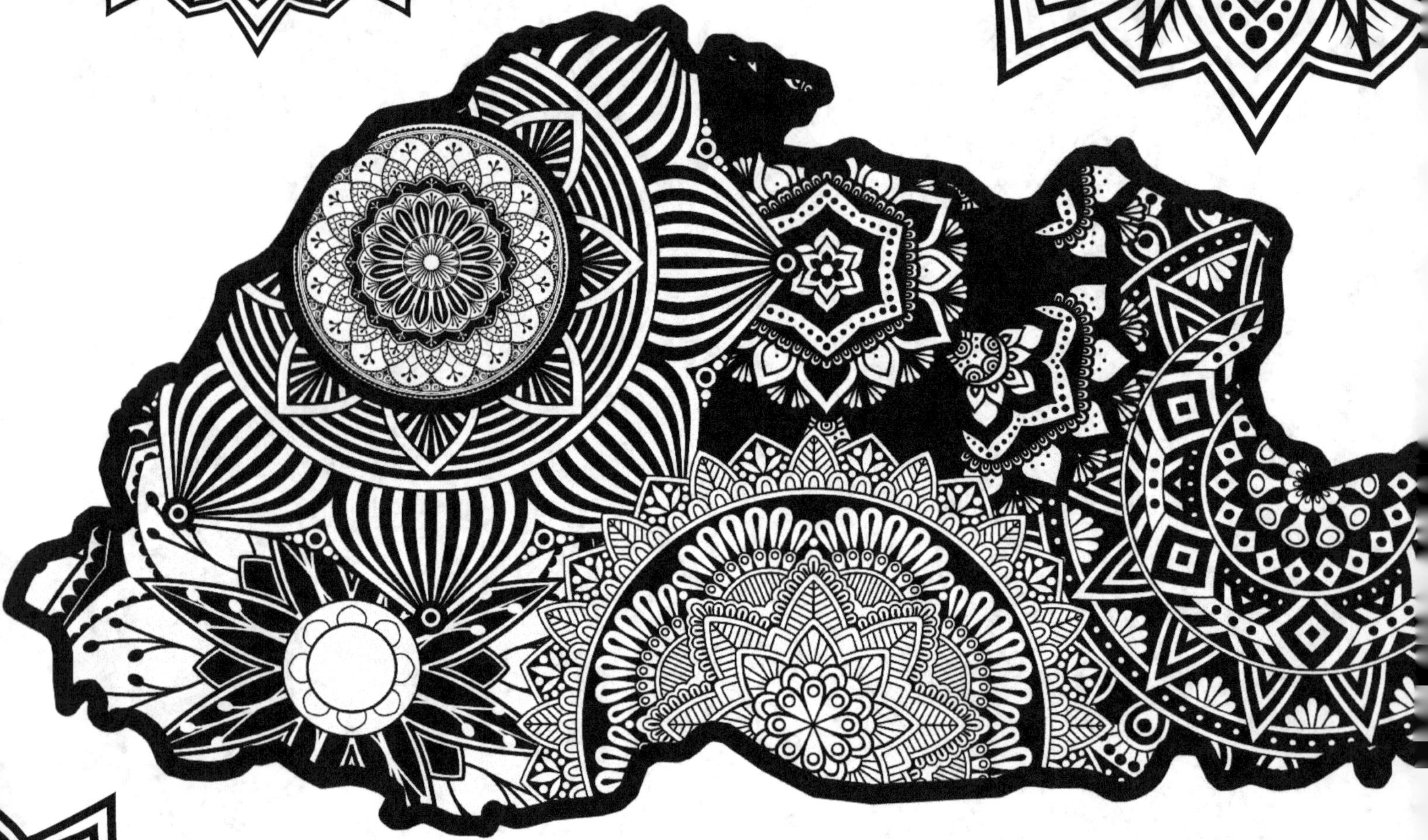

BHUTAN

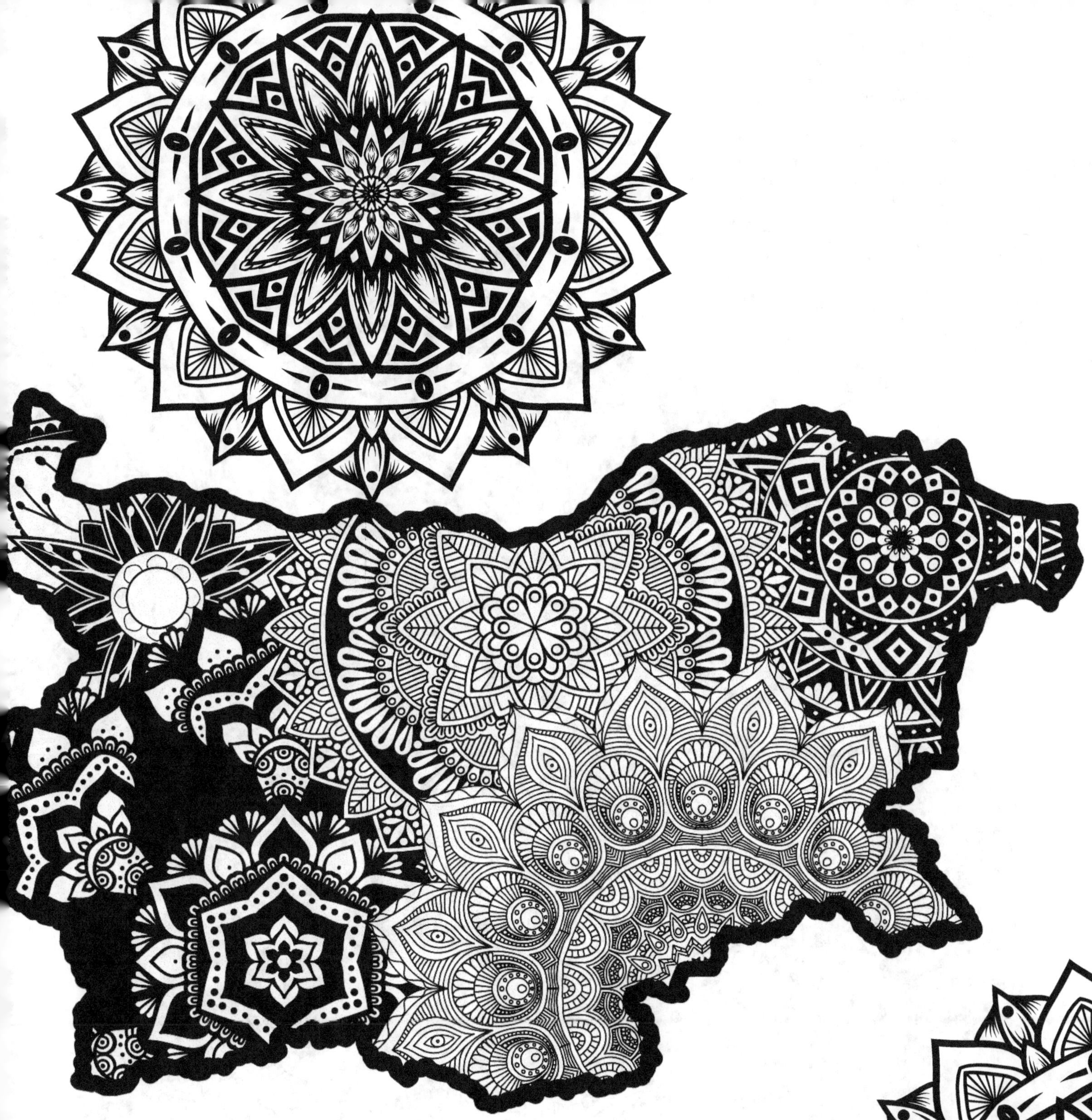

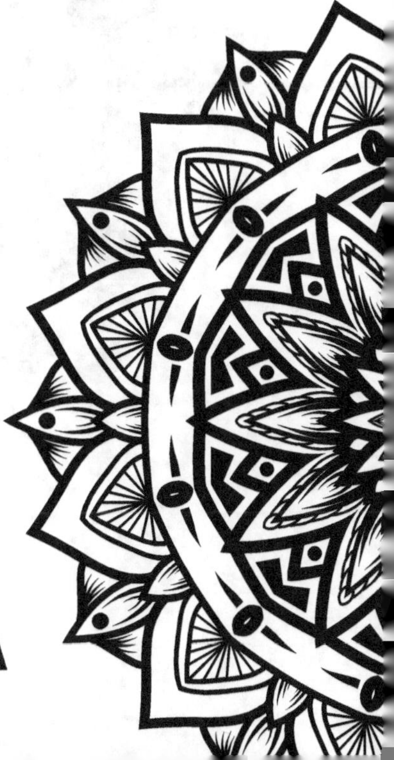

BULGARIA

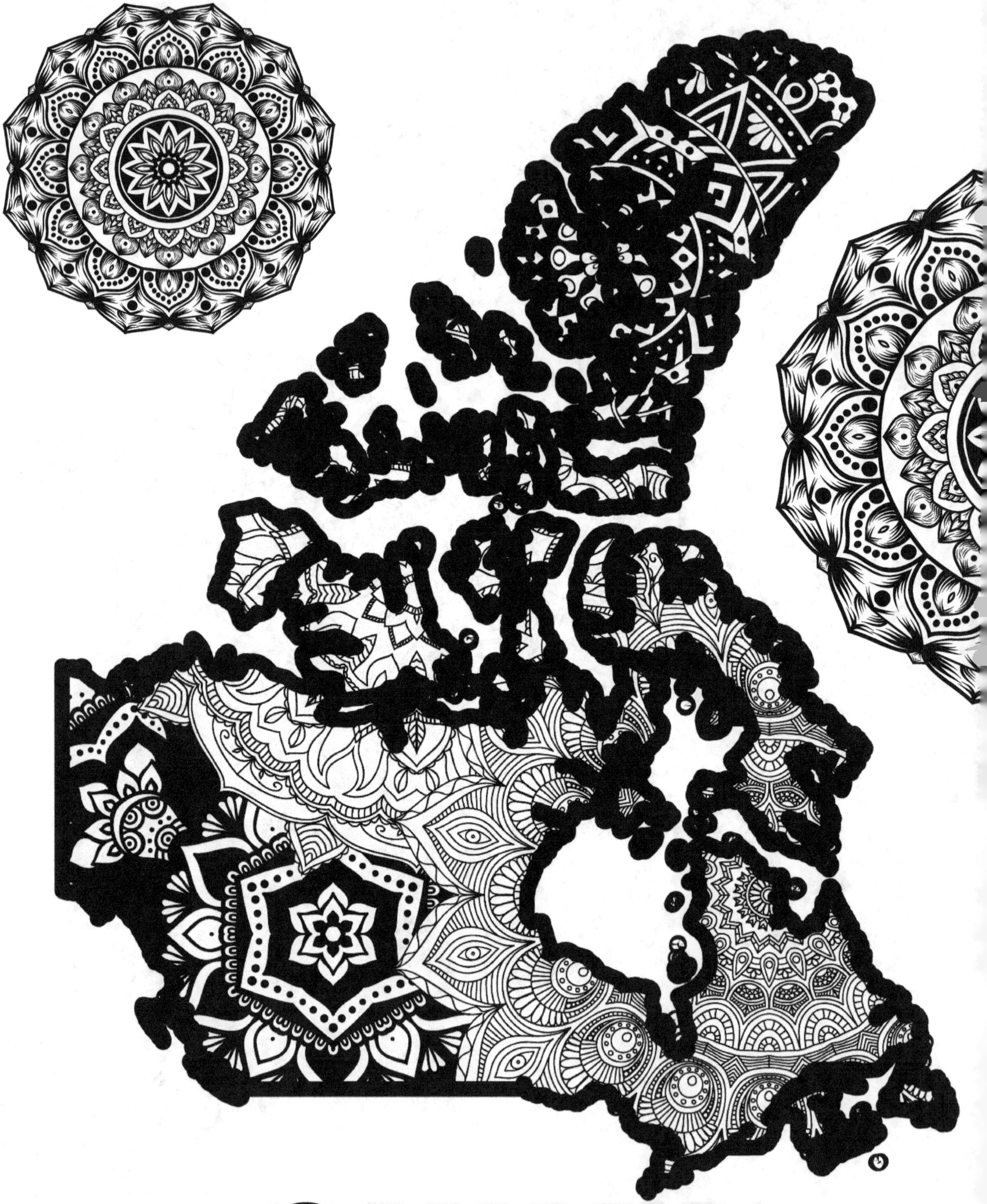

CANADA

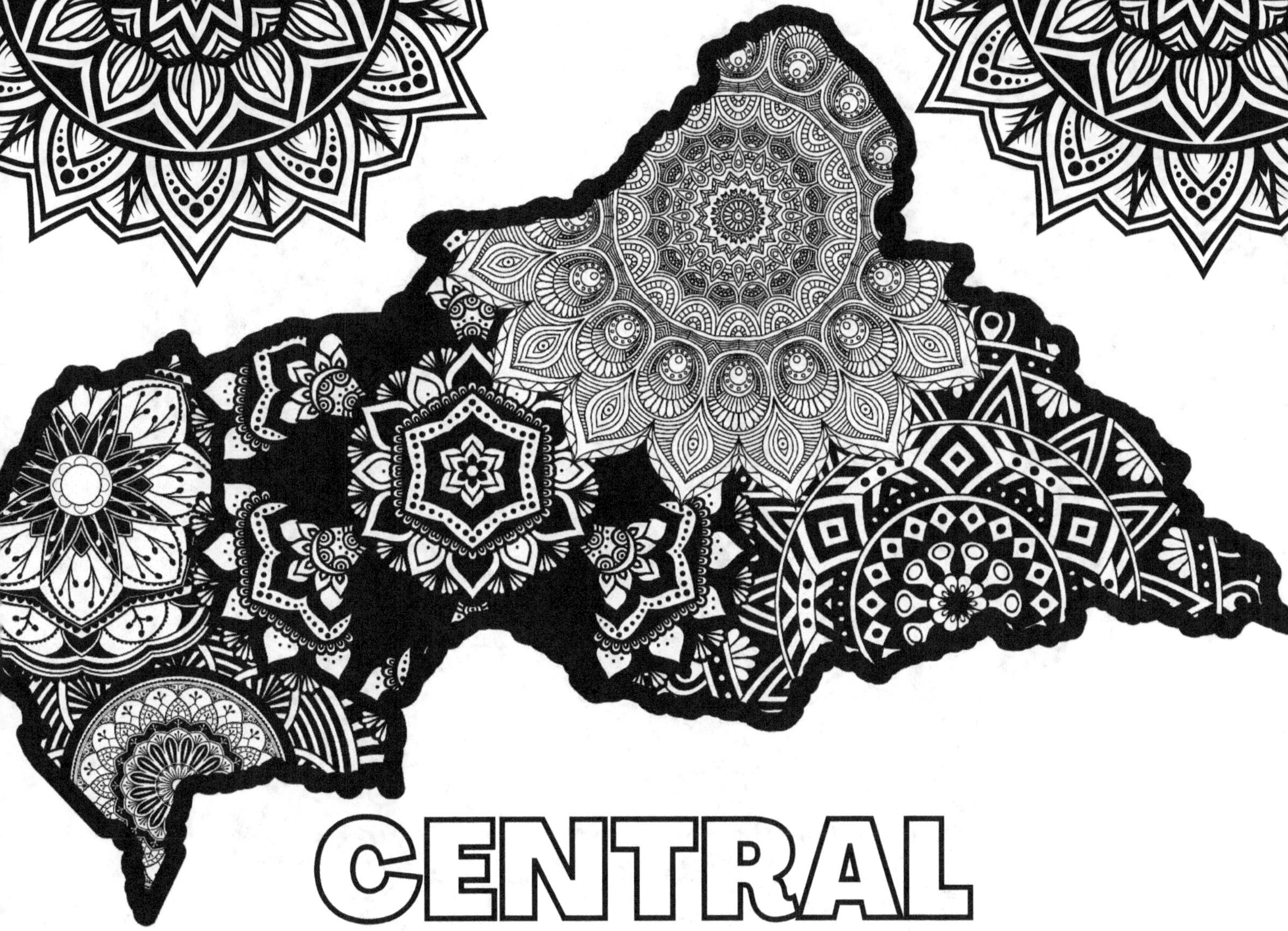

CENTRAL AFRICAN REPUBLIC

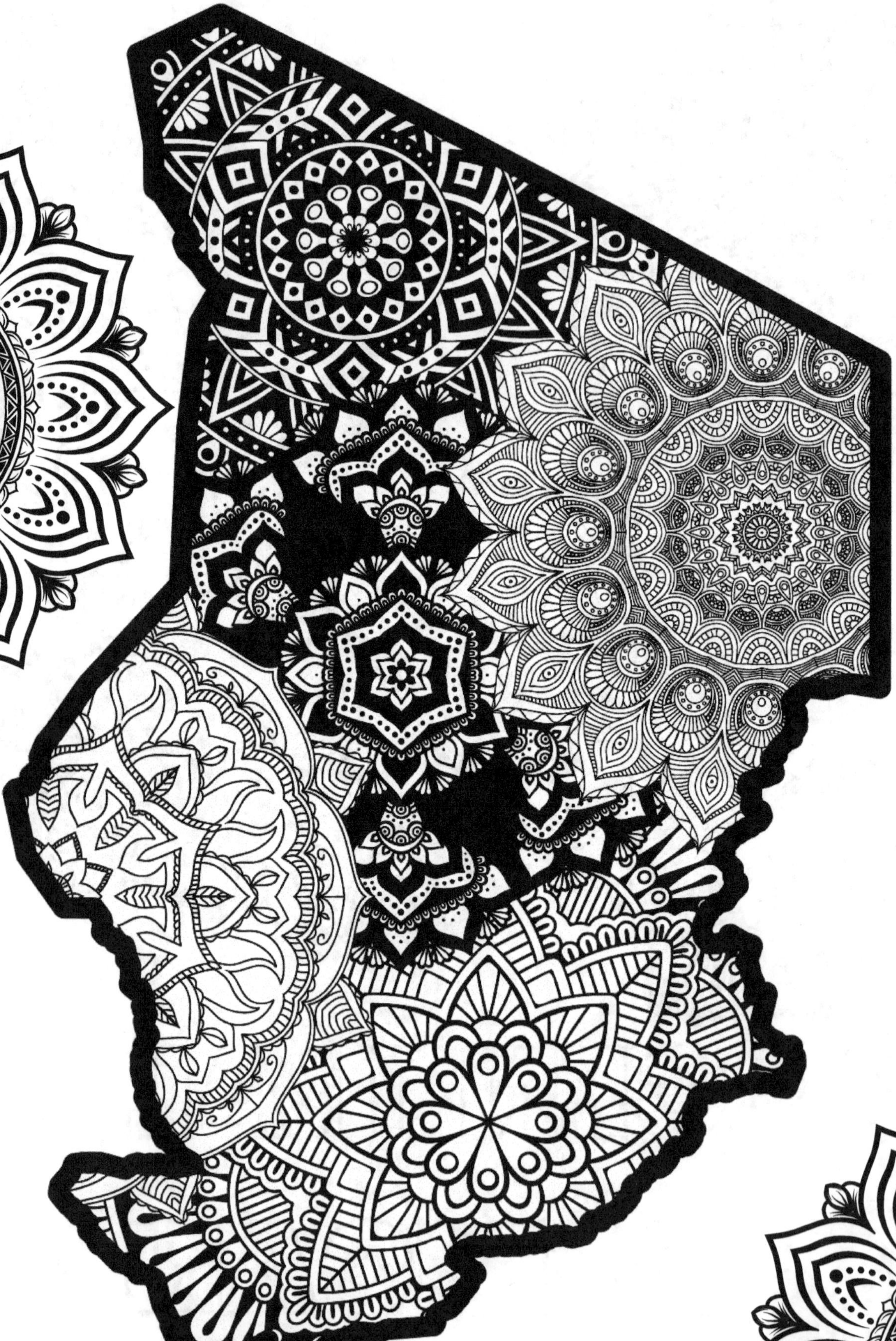

CHAD

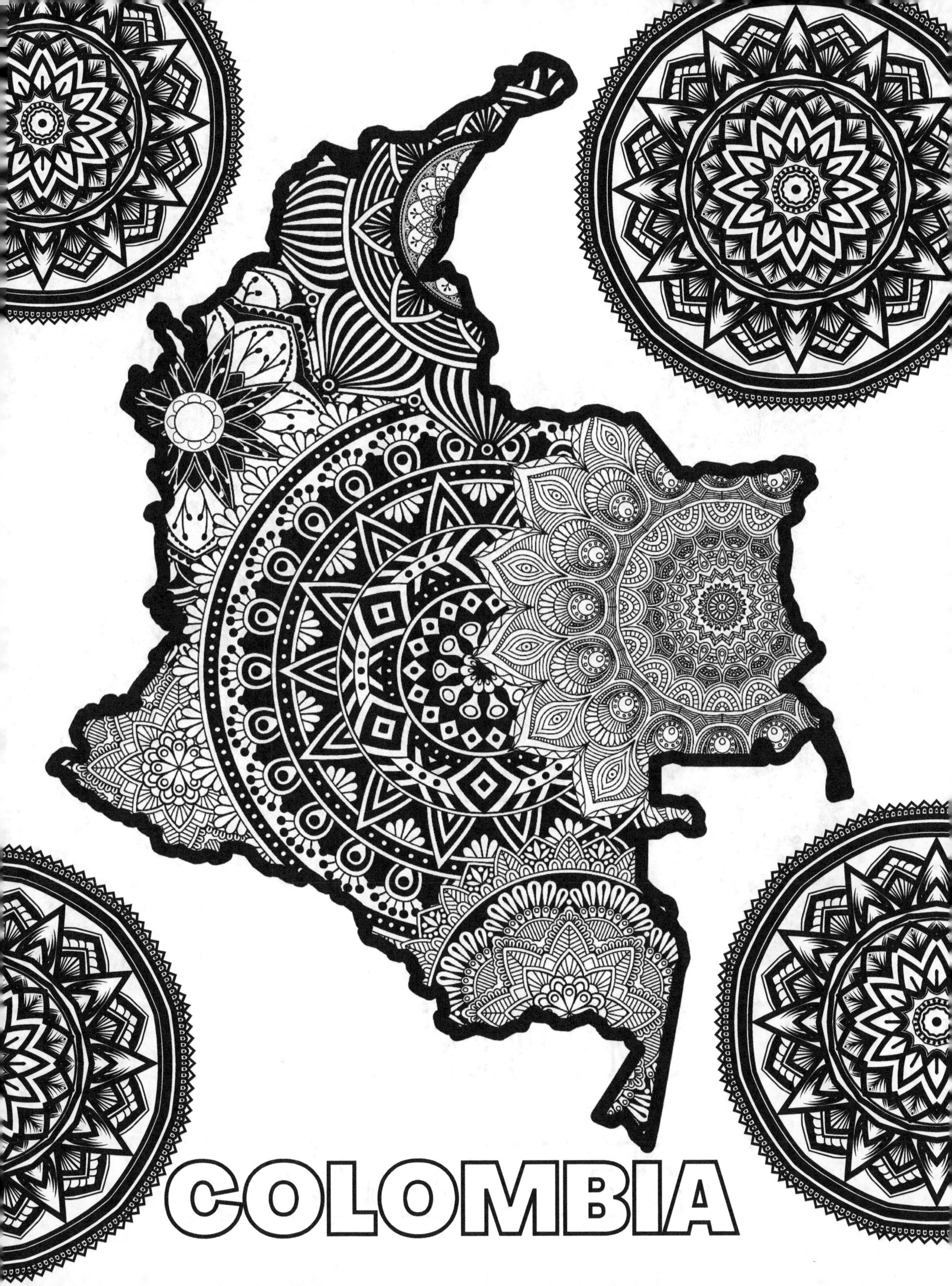
COLOMBIA

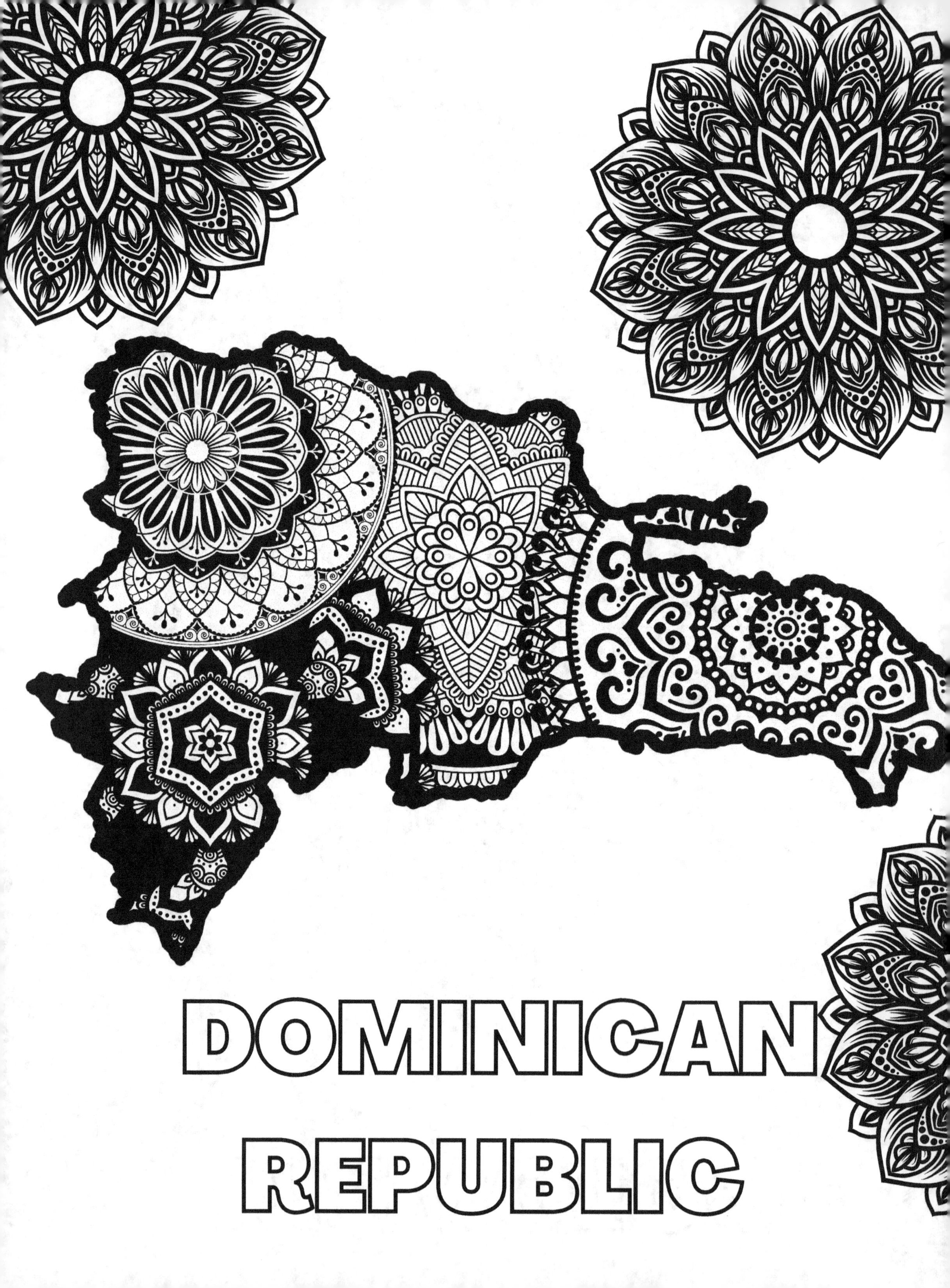
DOMINICAN
REPUBLIC

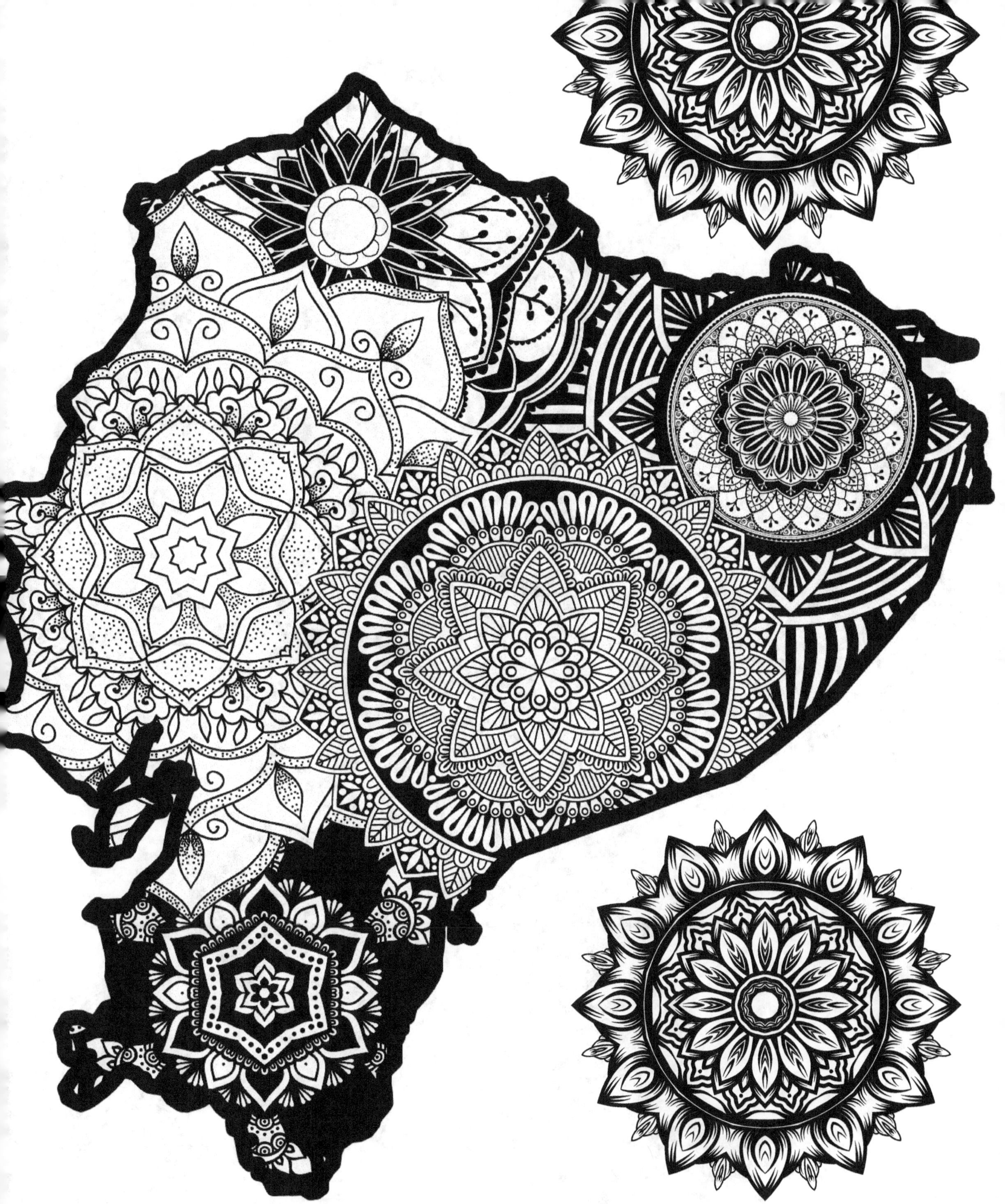

ECUADOR

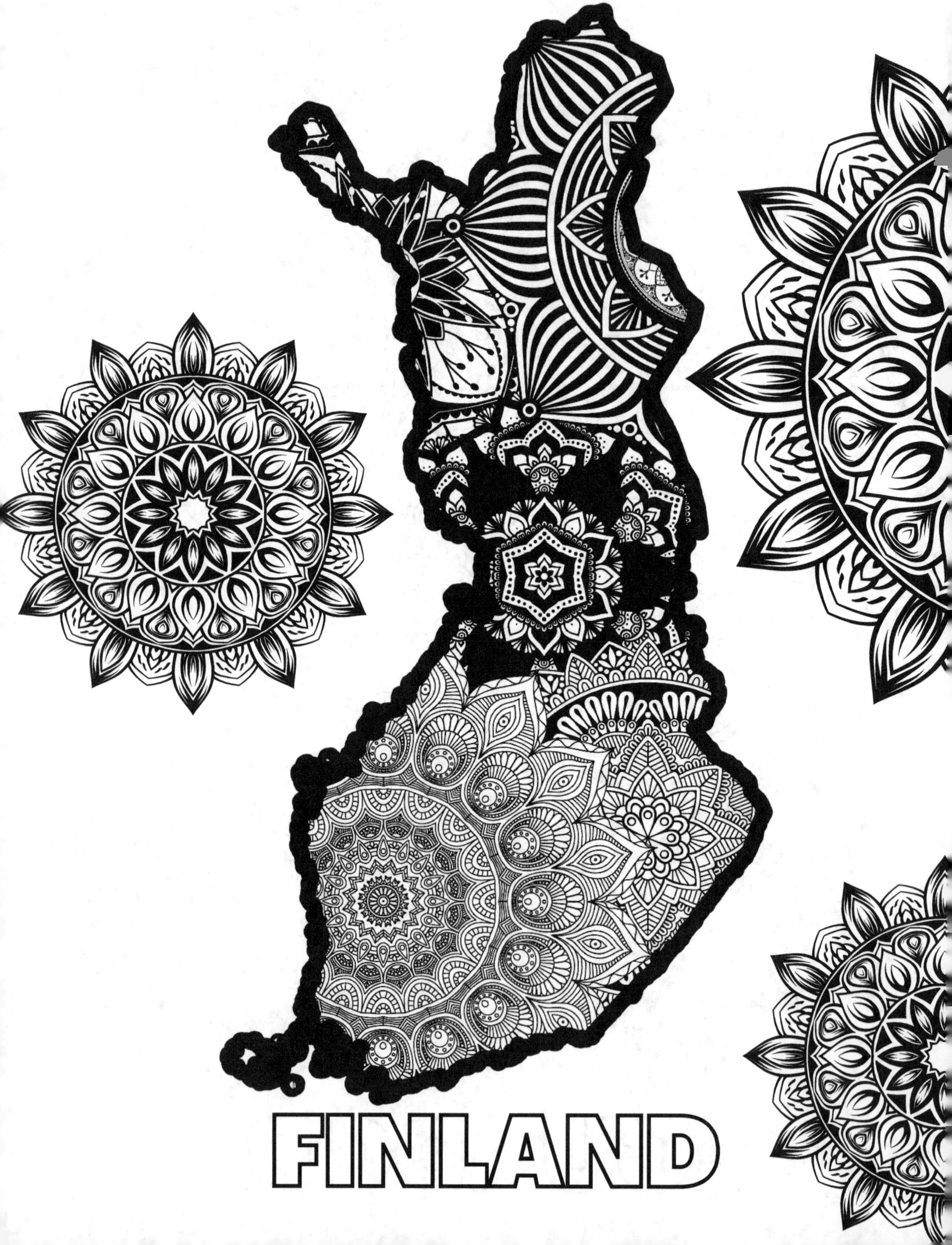

FINLAND

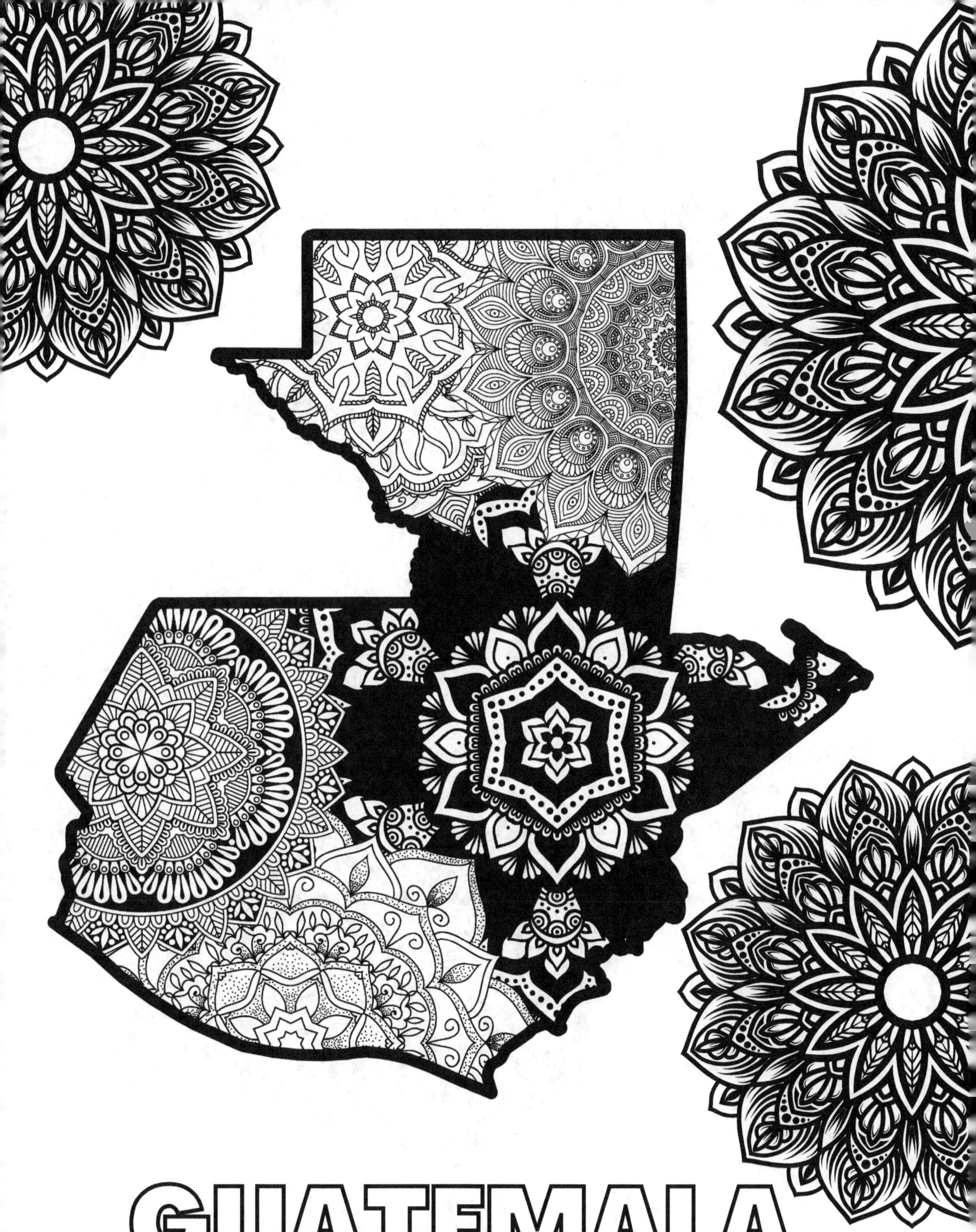

GUATEMALA

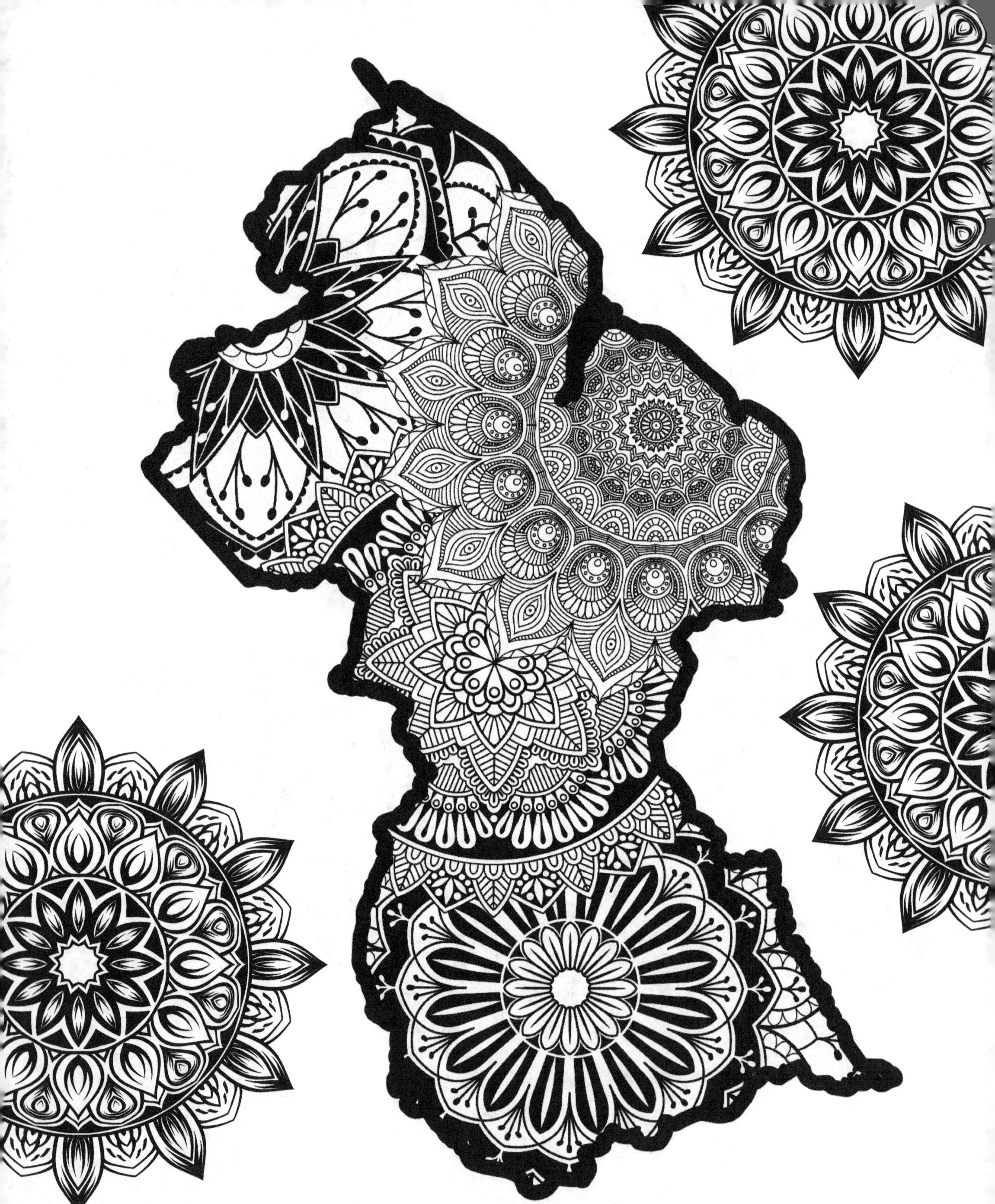

GUYANA

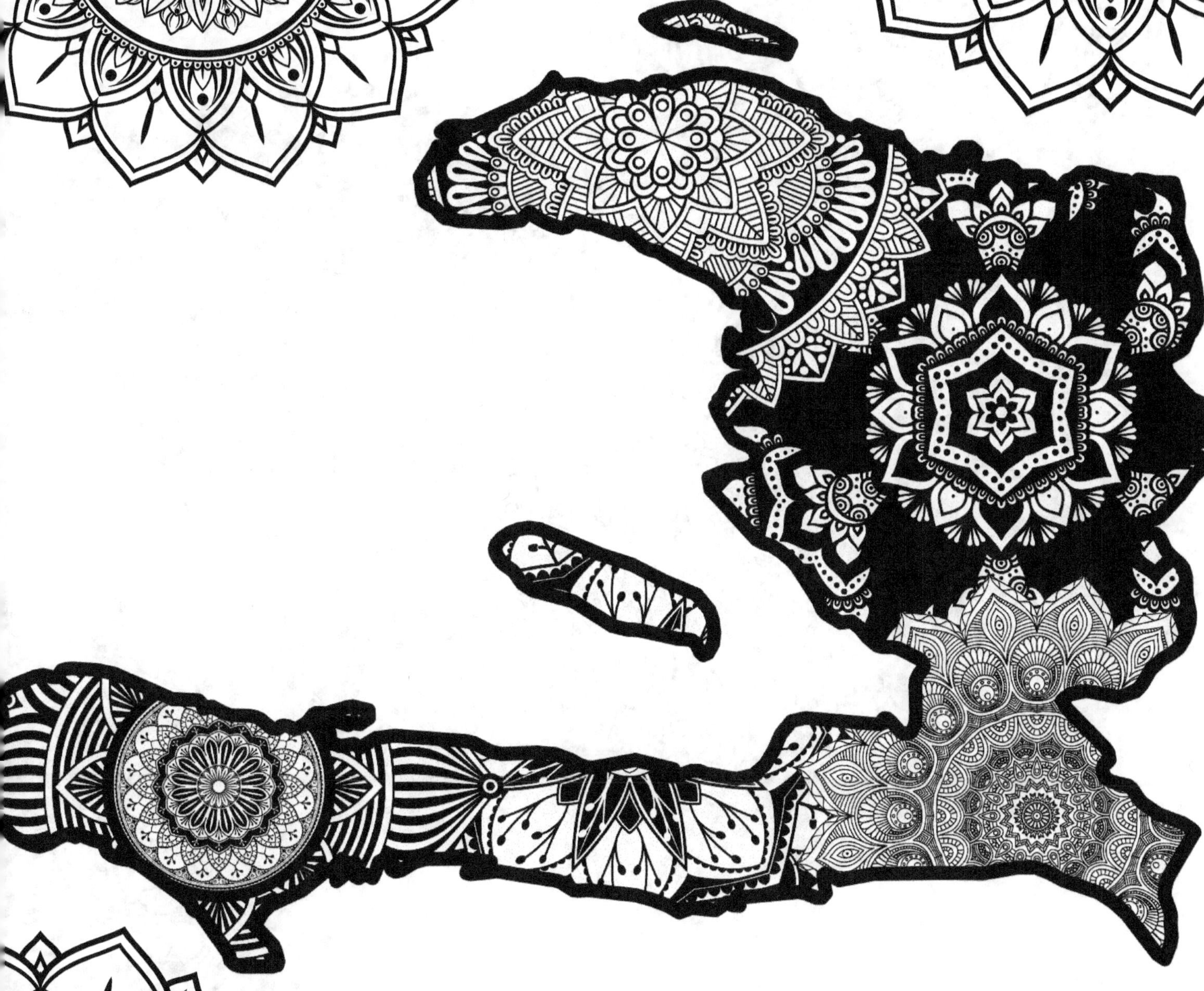

HAITI

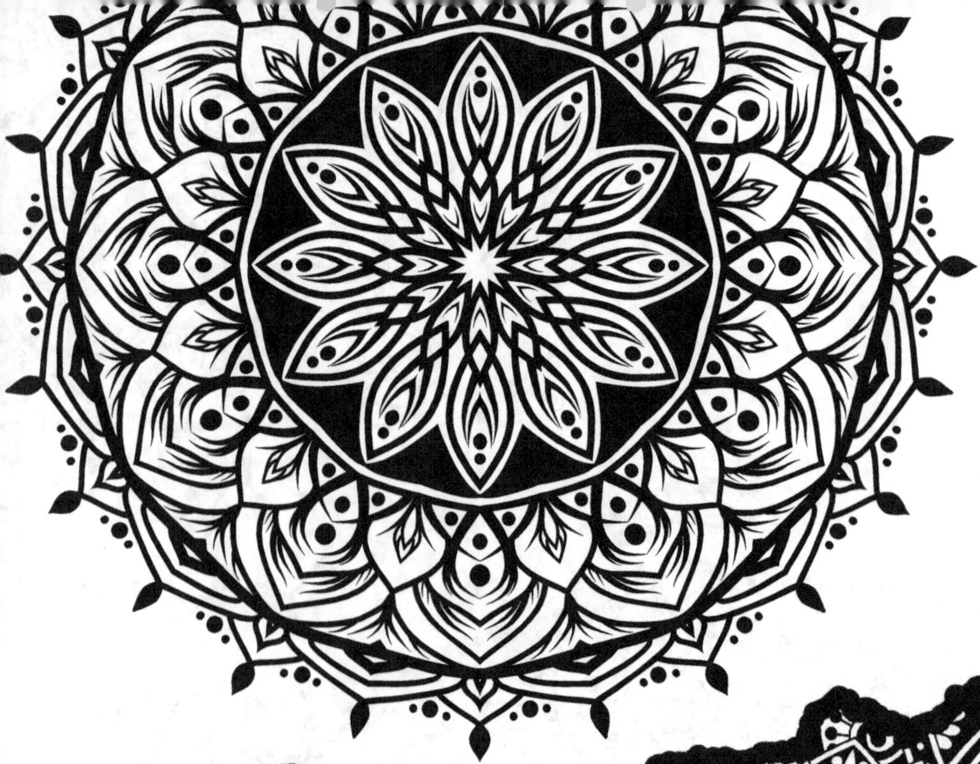

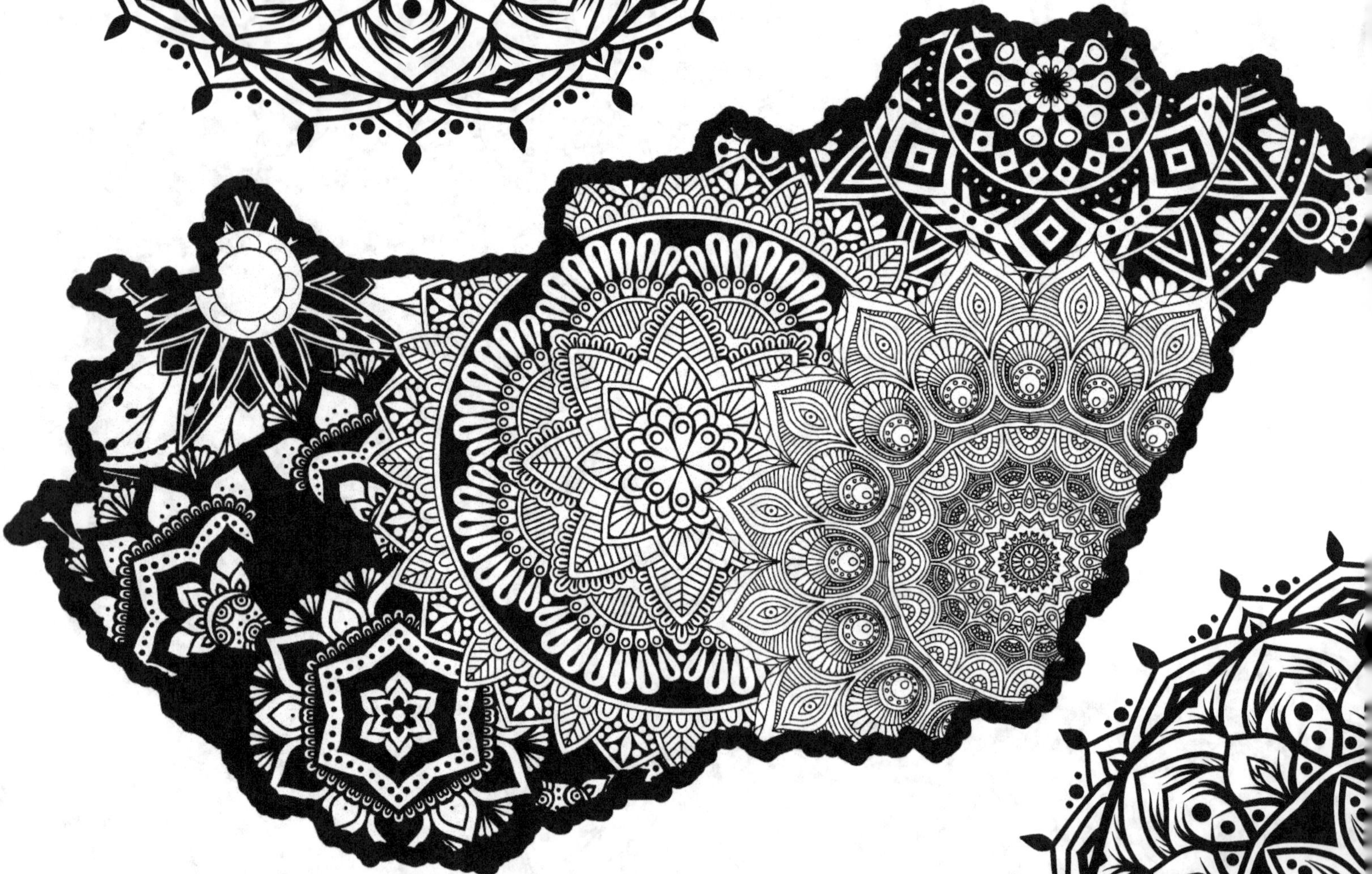

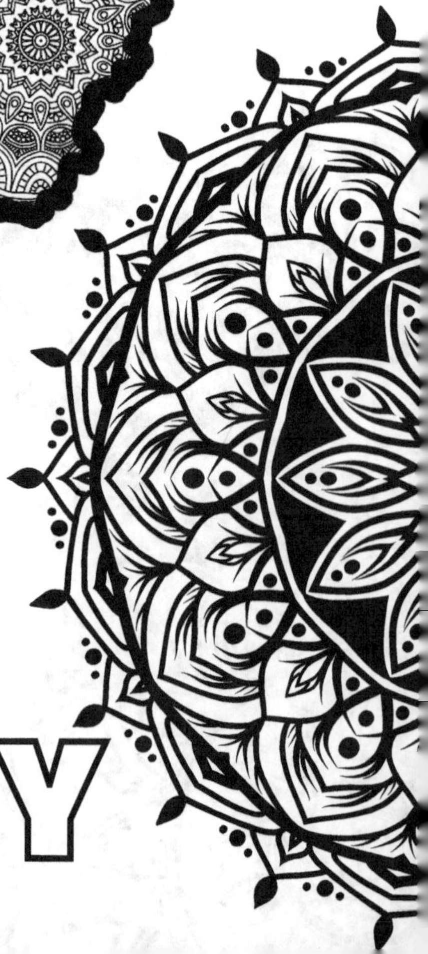

HUNGARY

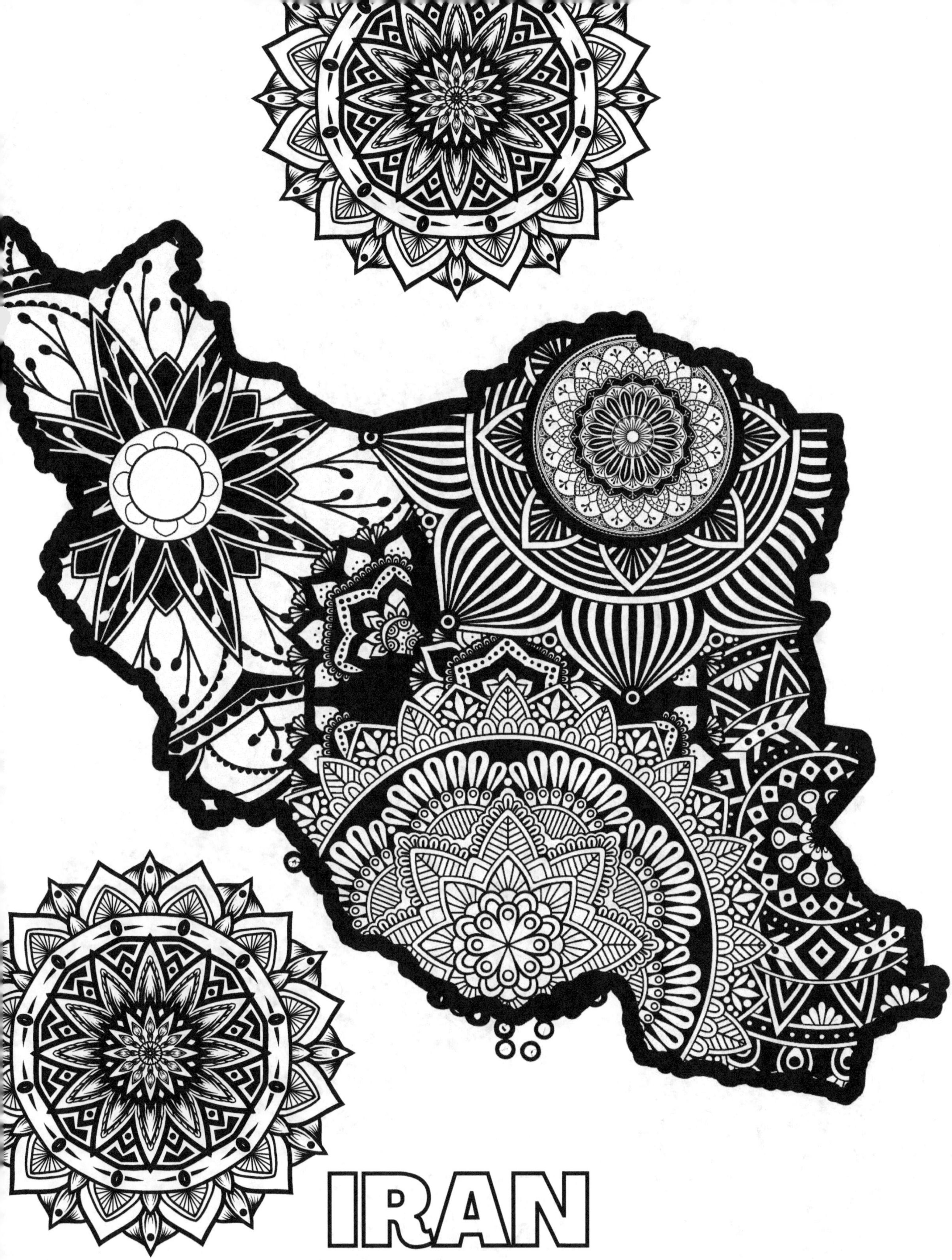
IRAN

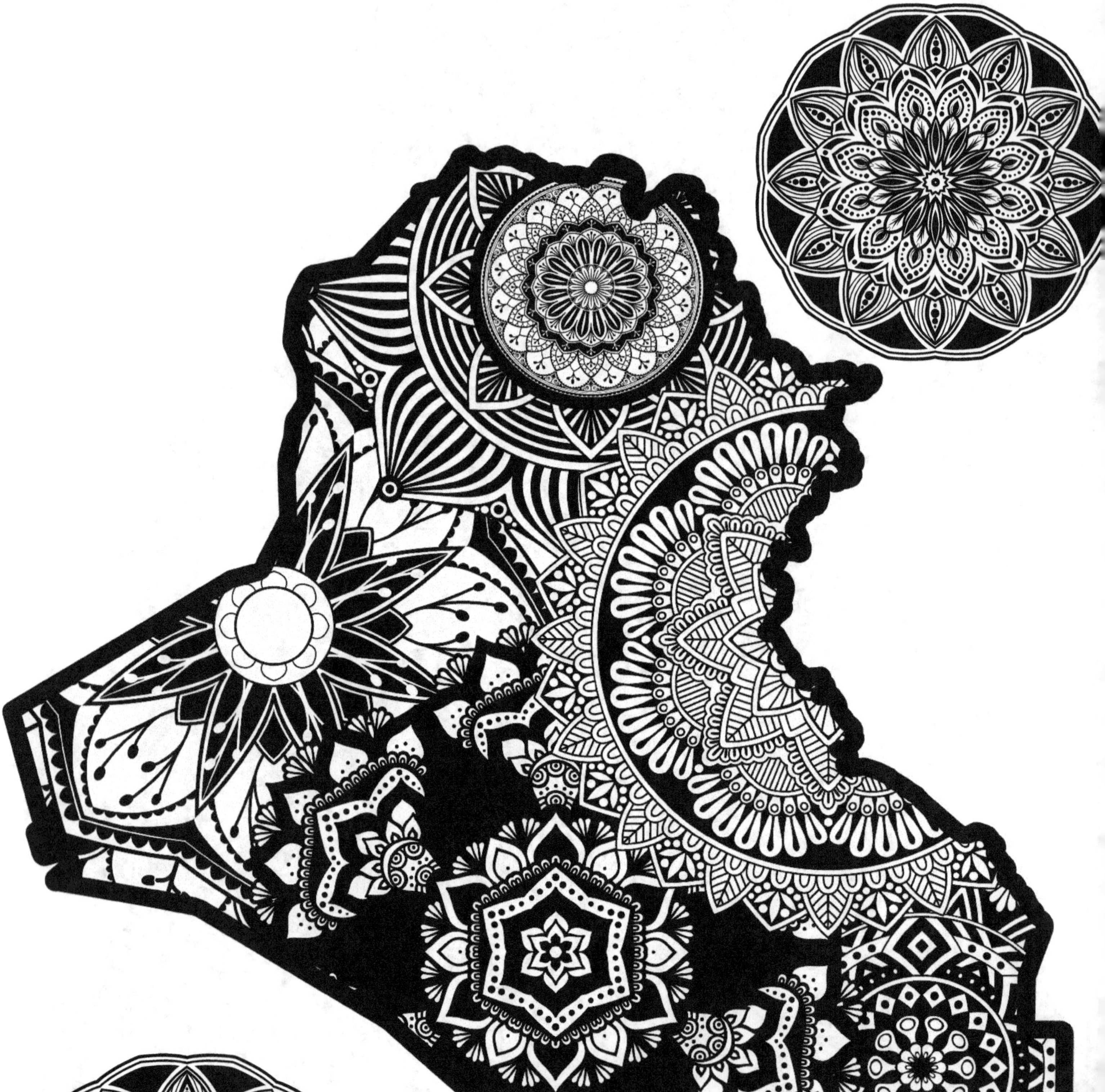

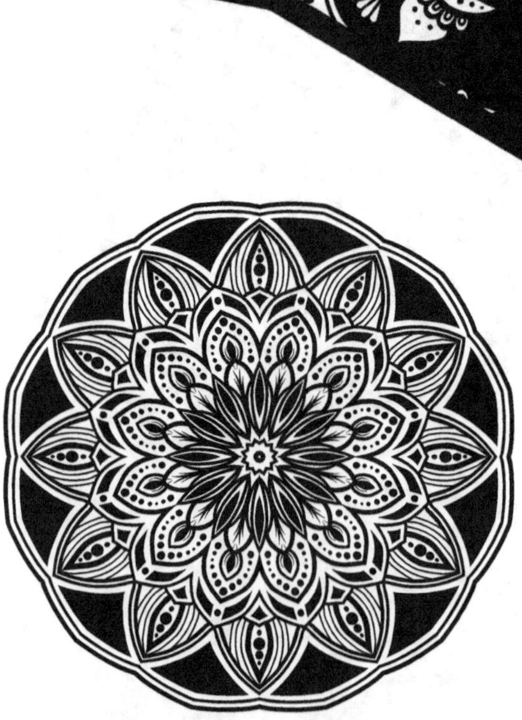

IRAQ

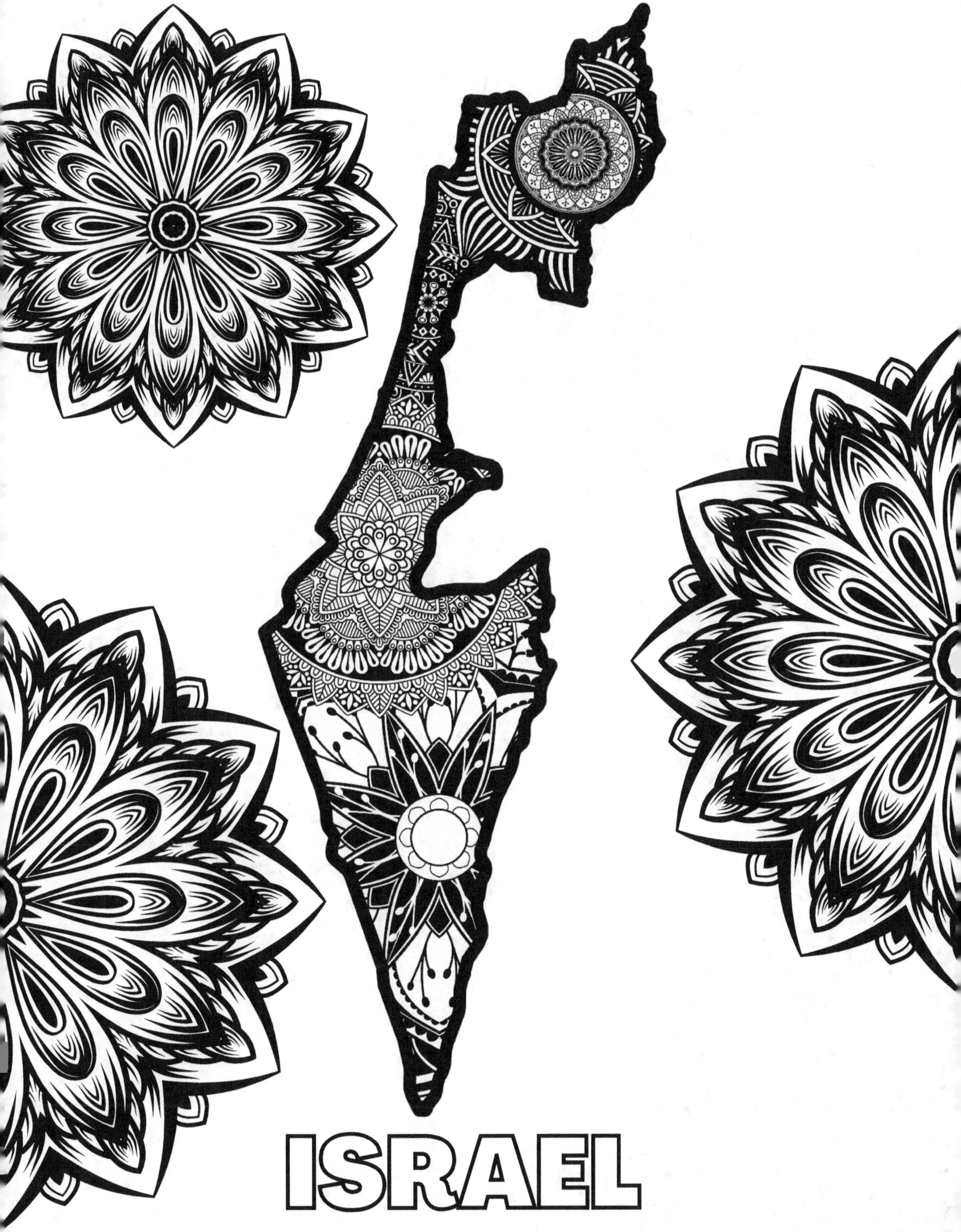
ISRAEL

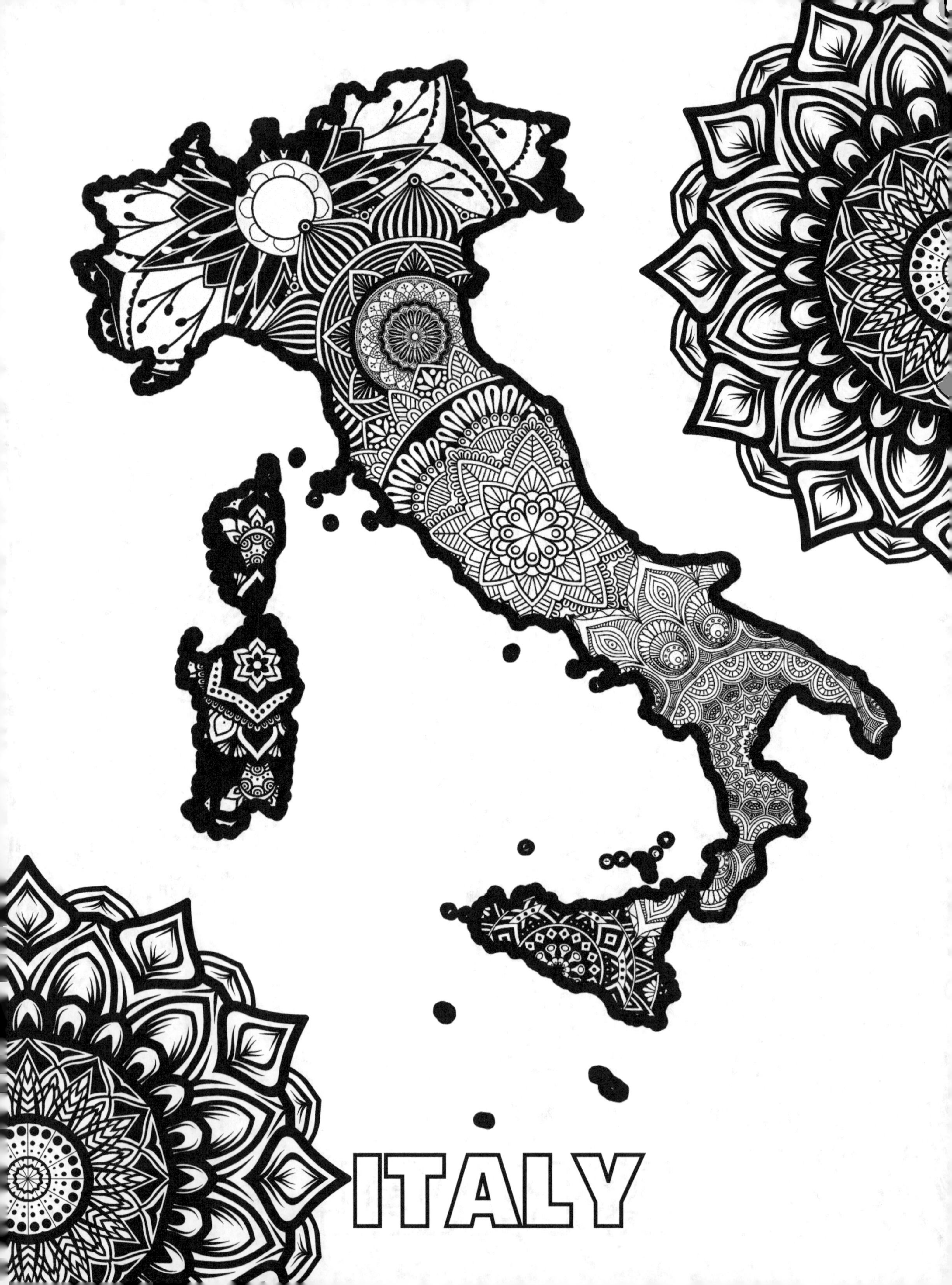
ITALY

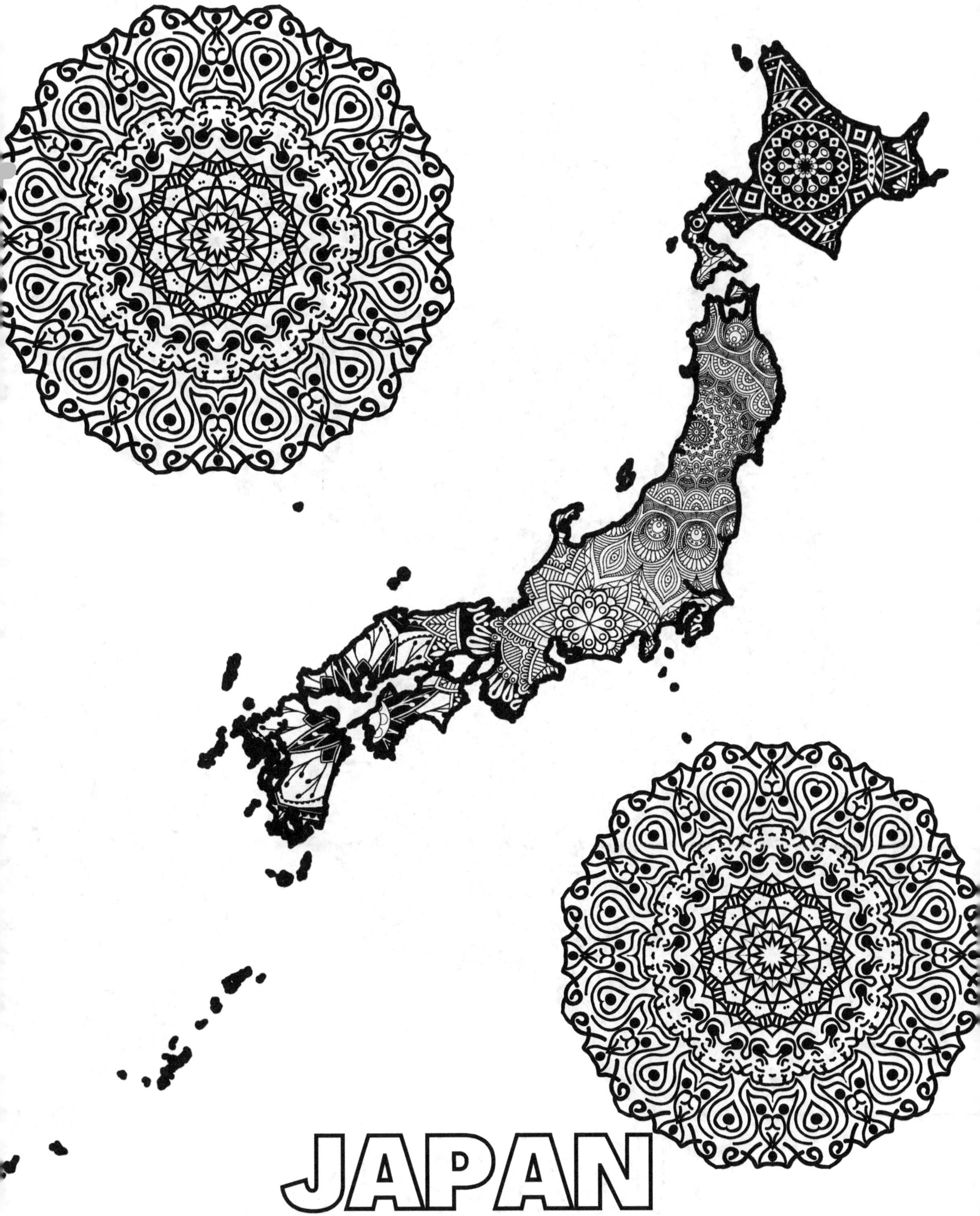

JAPAN

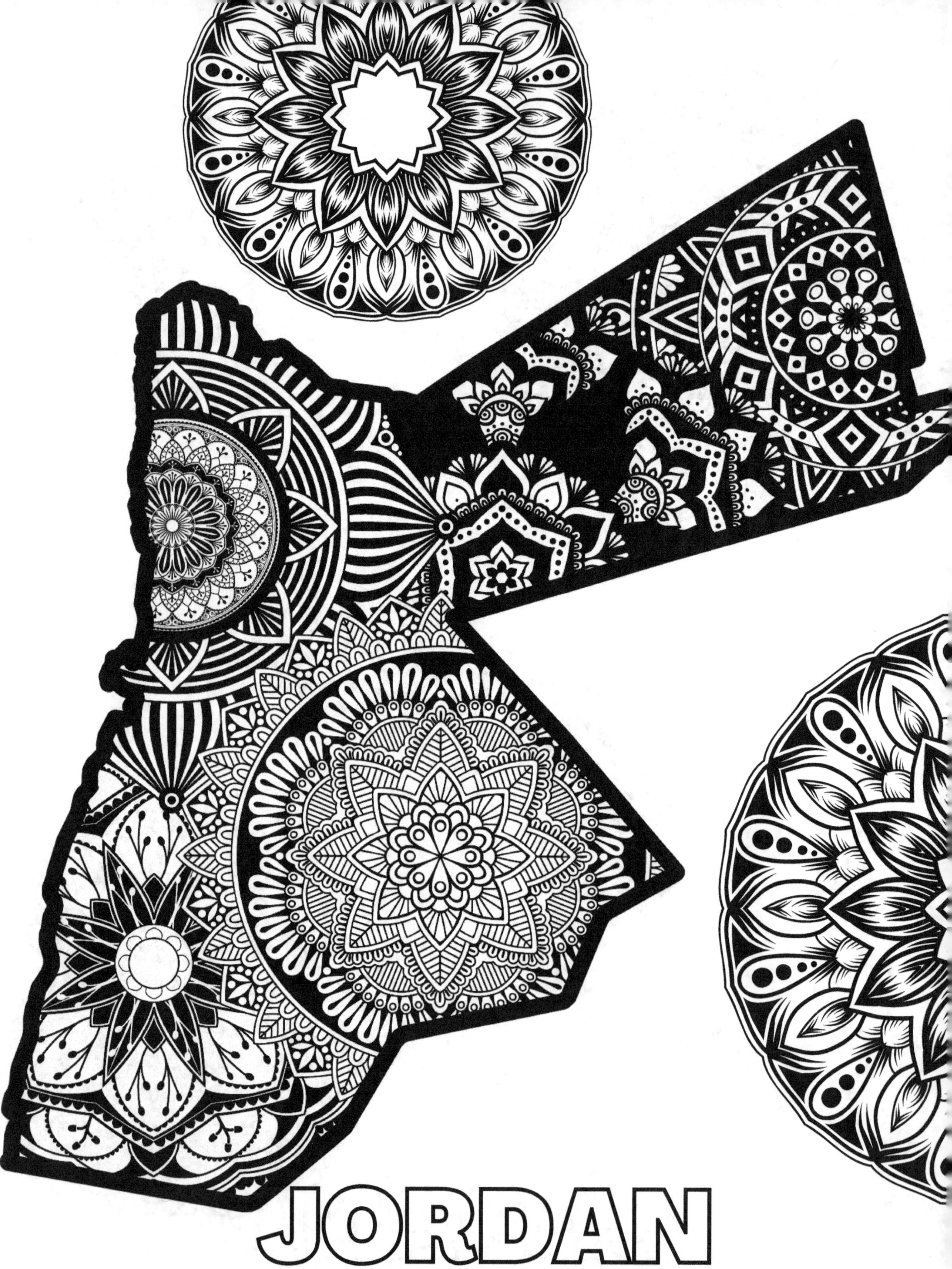

JORDAN

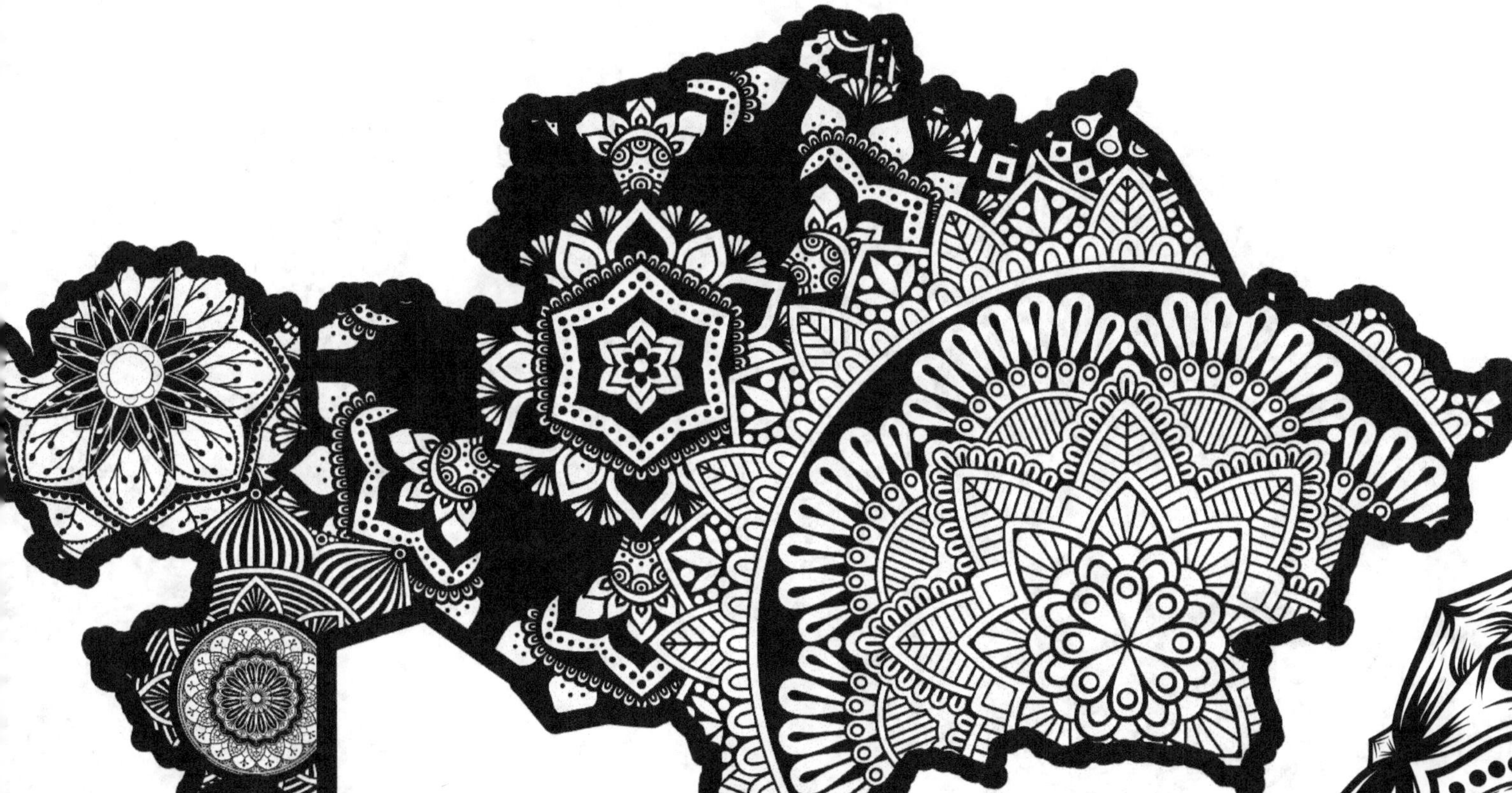

KAZAKHSTAN

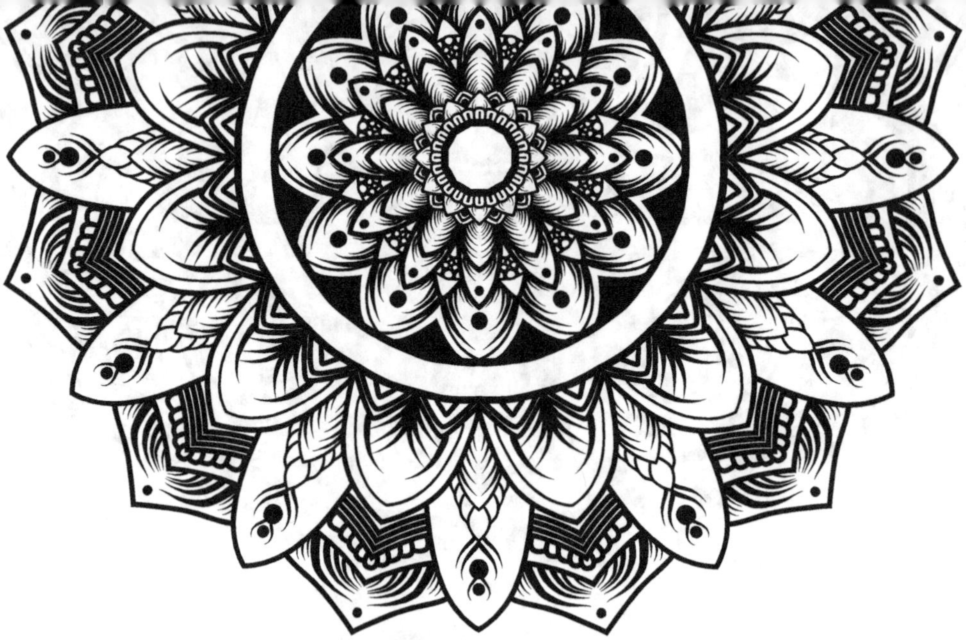

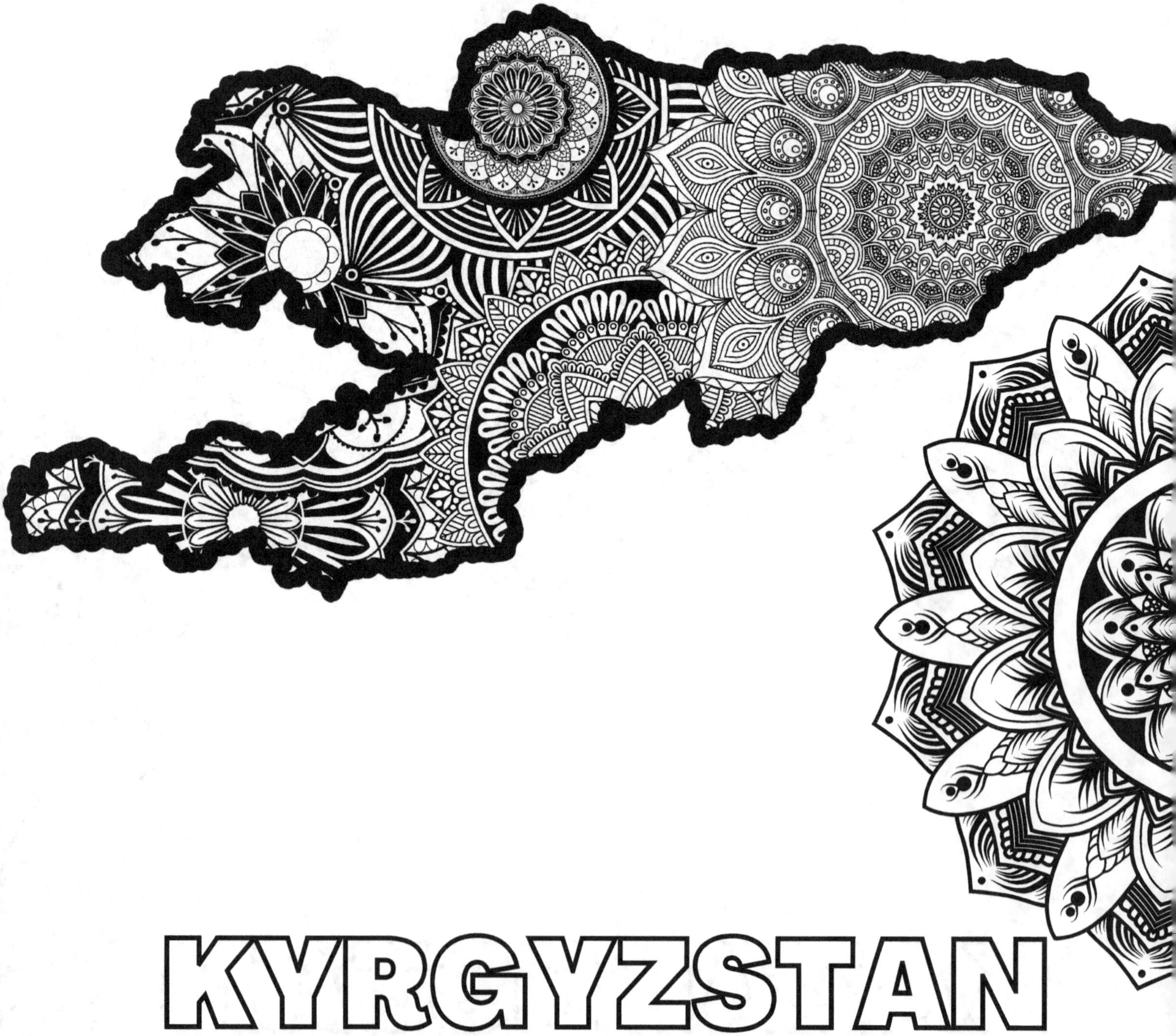

KYRGYZSTAN

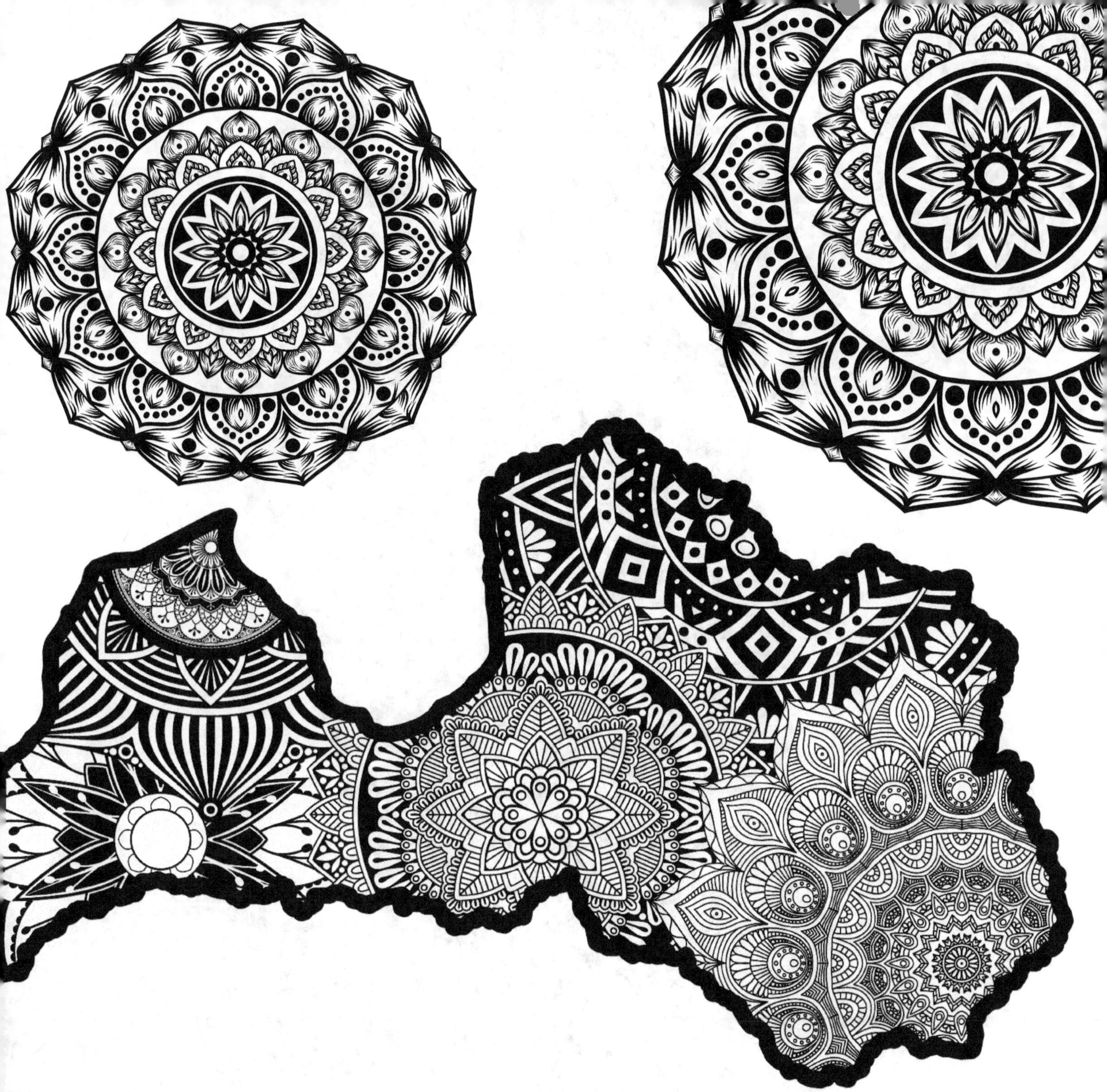

LATVIA

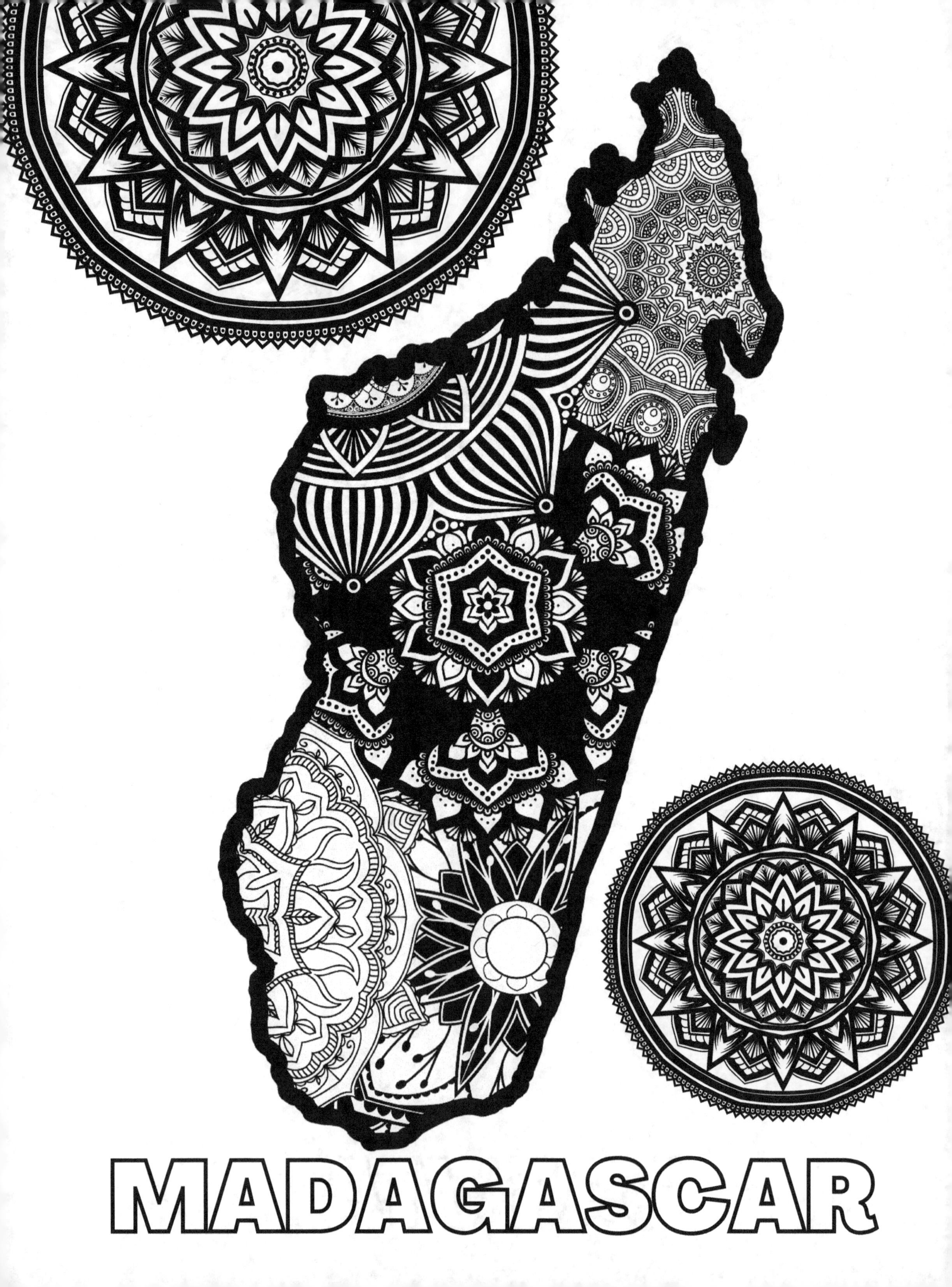
MADAGASCAR

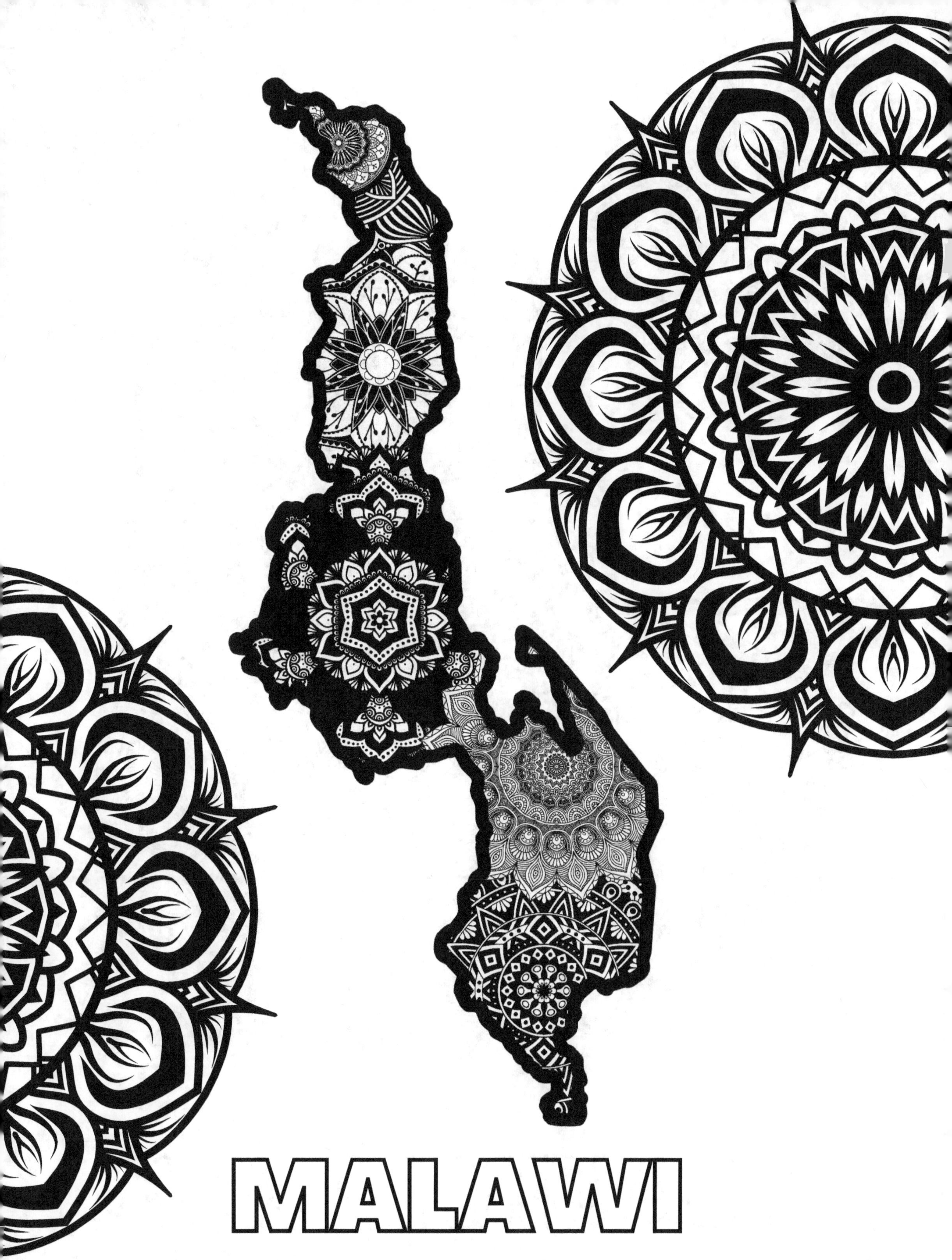

MALAWI

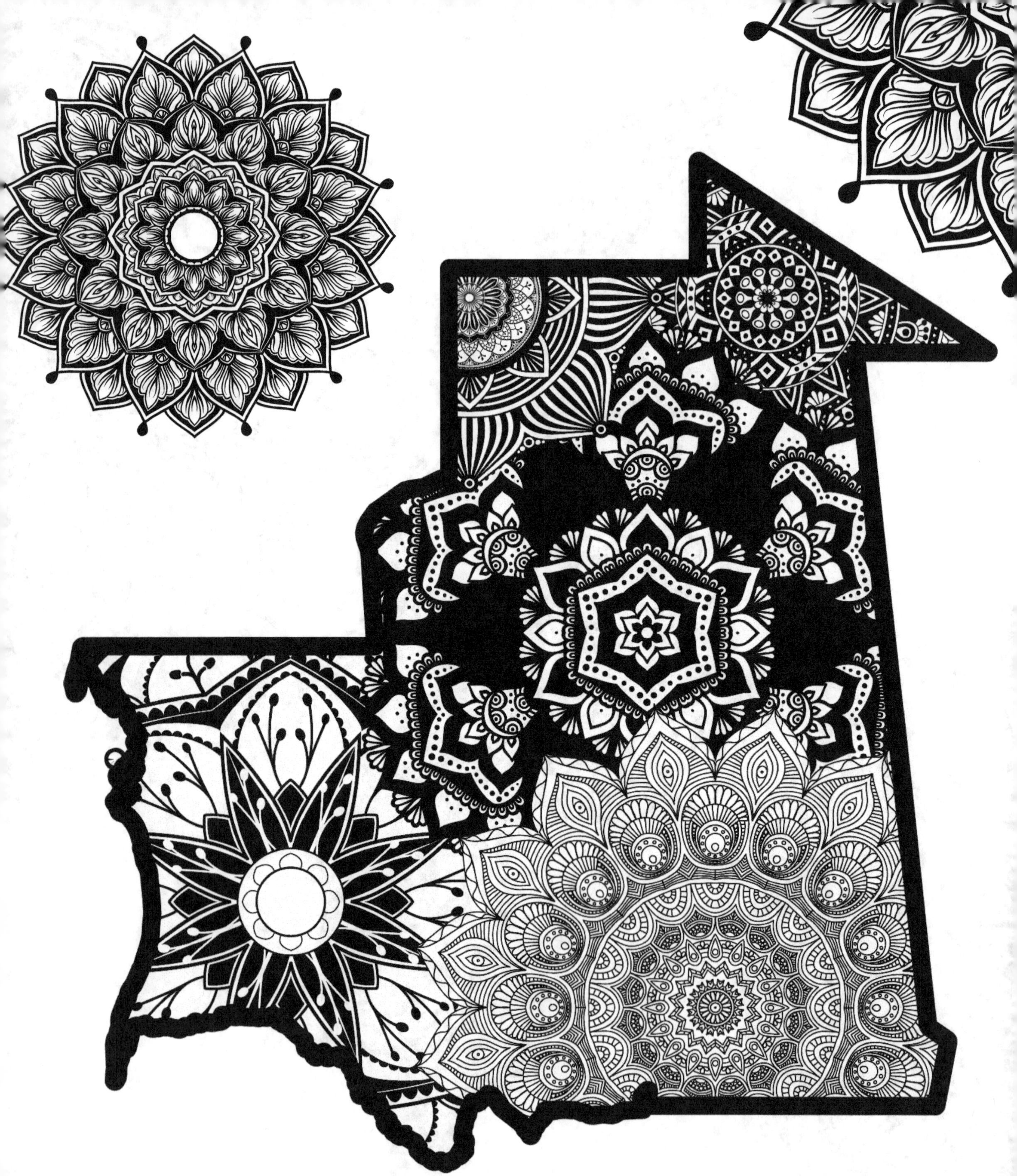

MAURITANIA

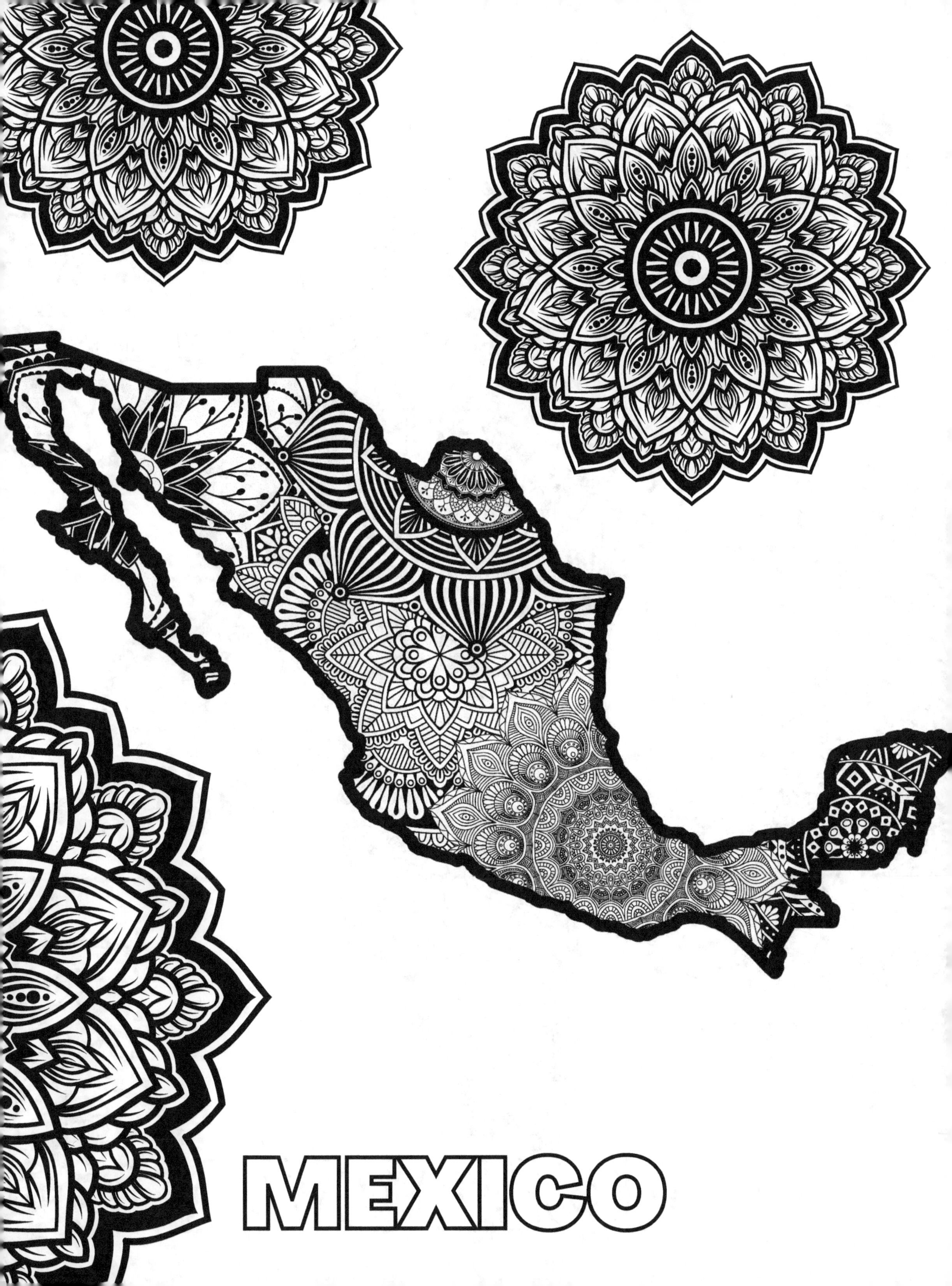

MEXICO

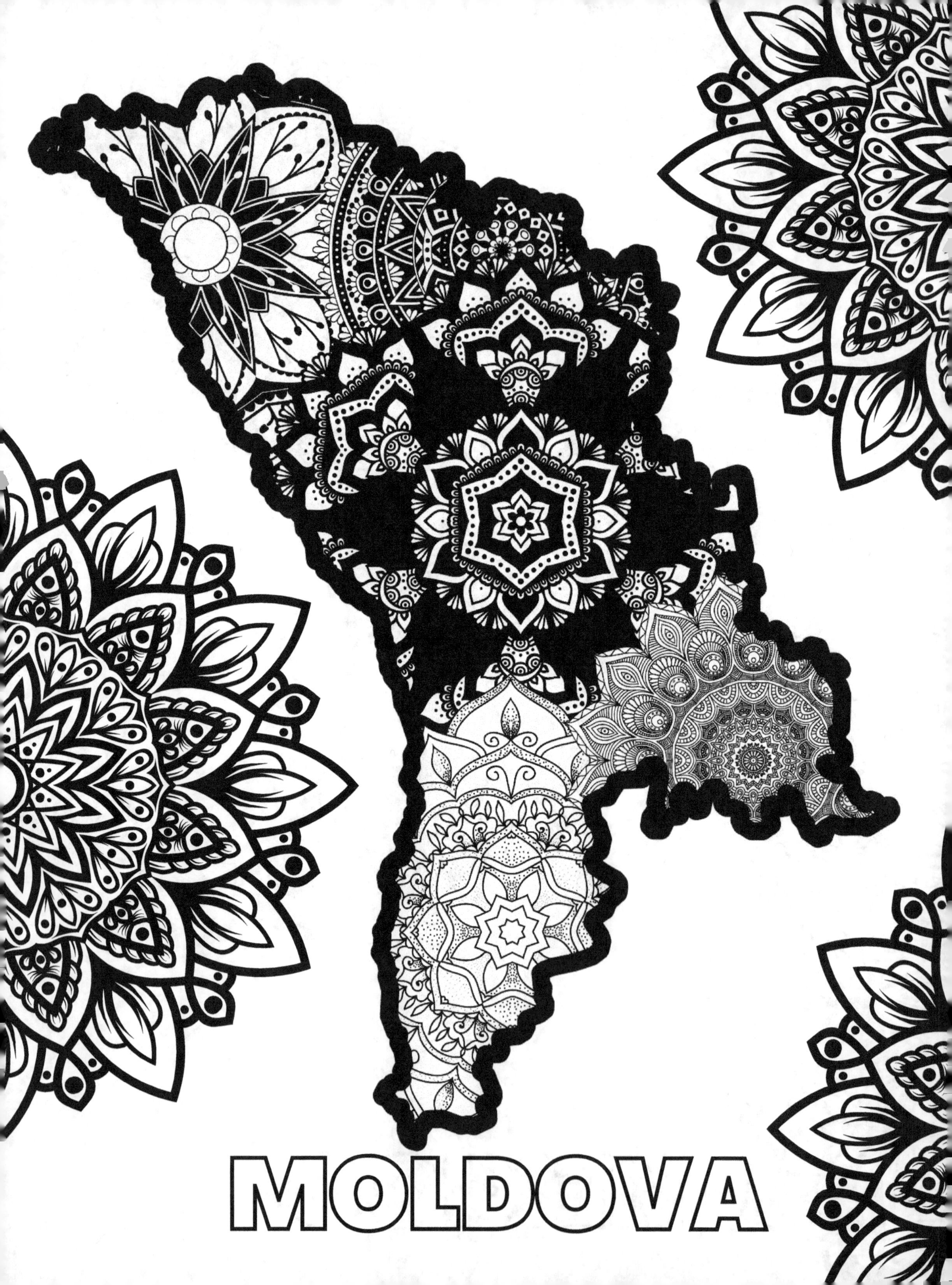
MOLDOVA

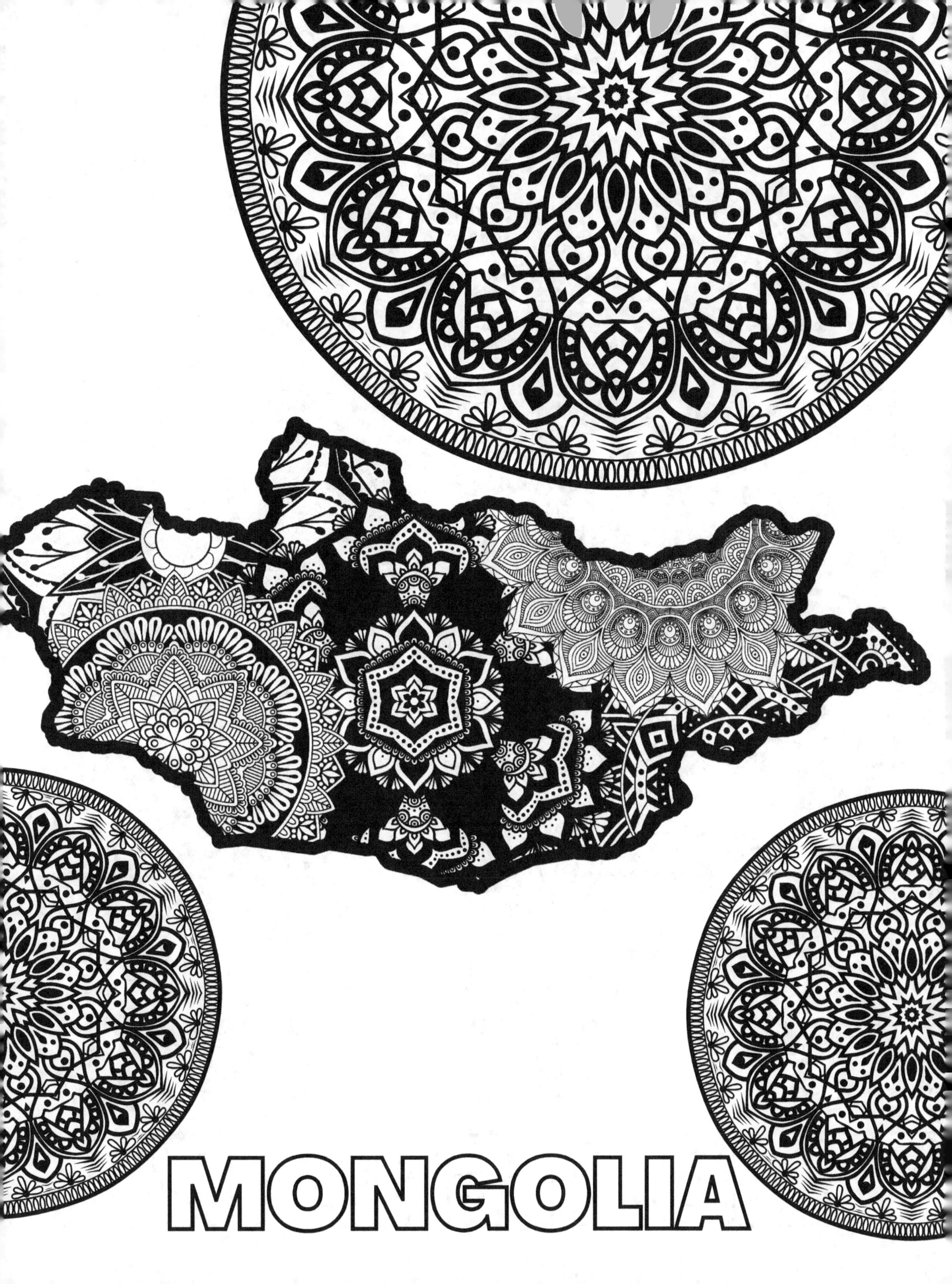
MONGOLIA

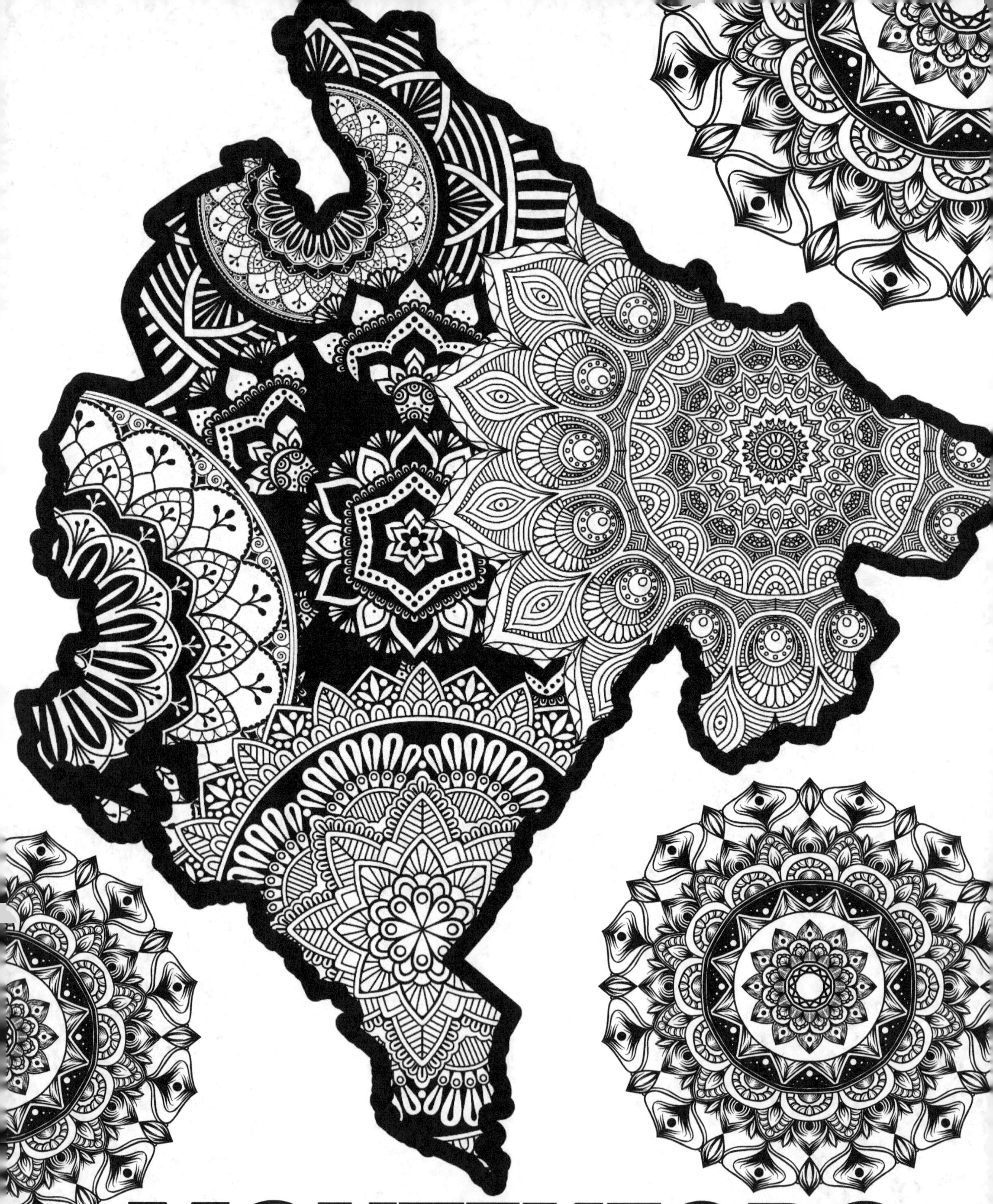

MONTENEGRO

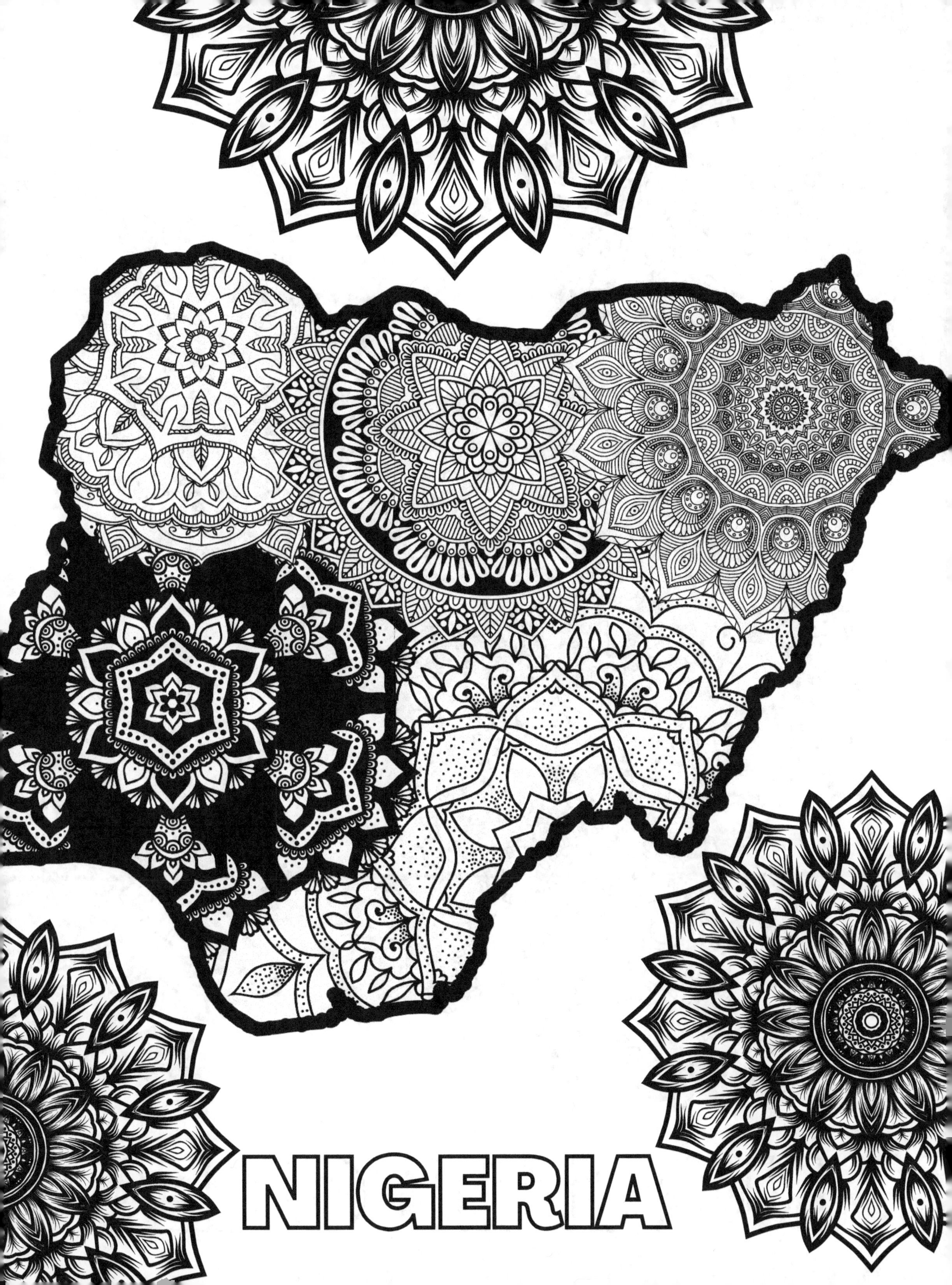
NIGERIA

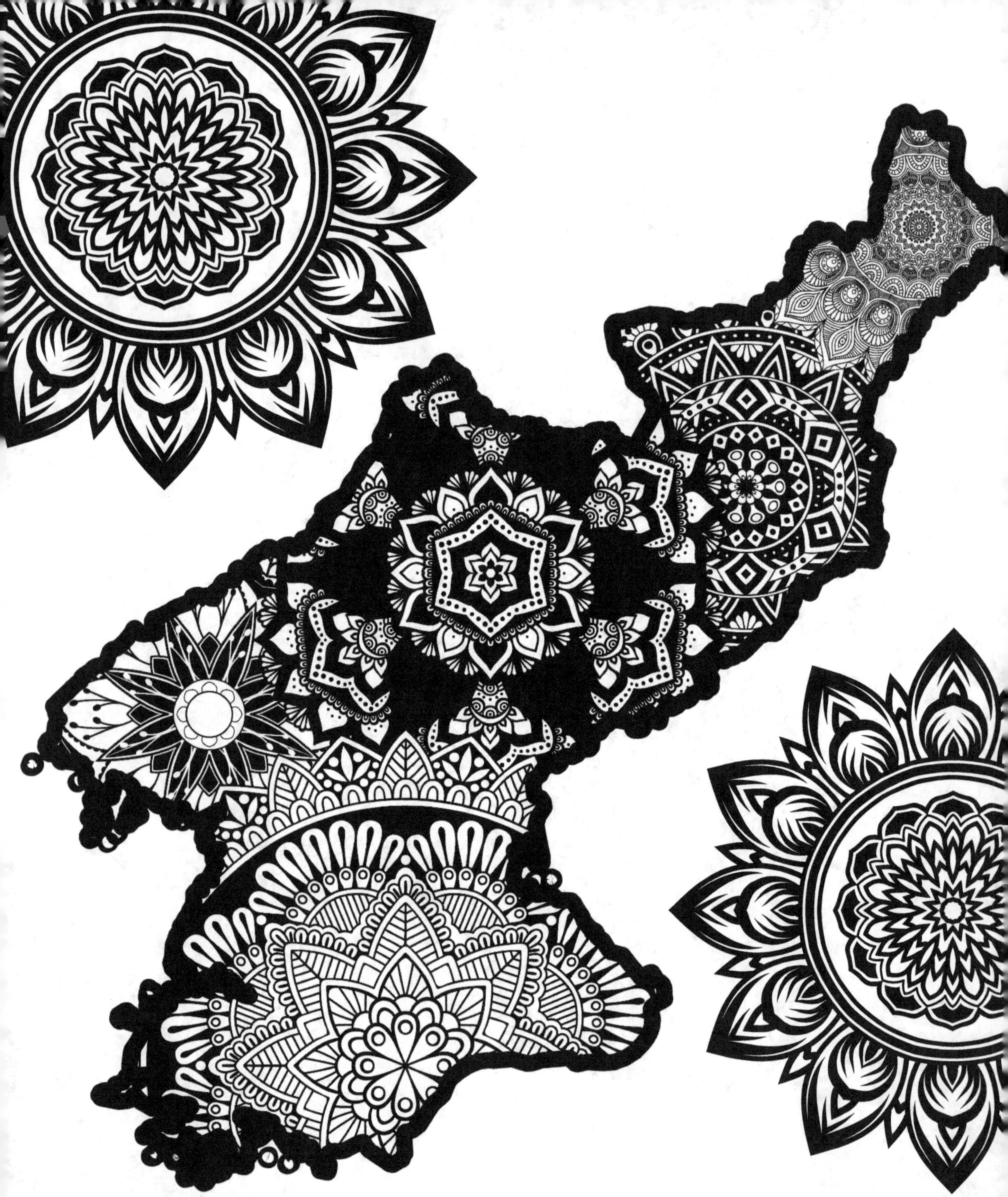

NORTH KOREA

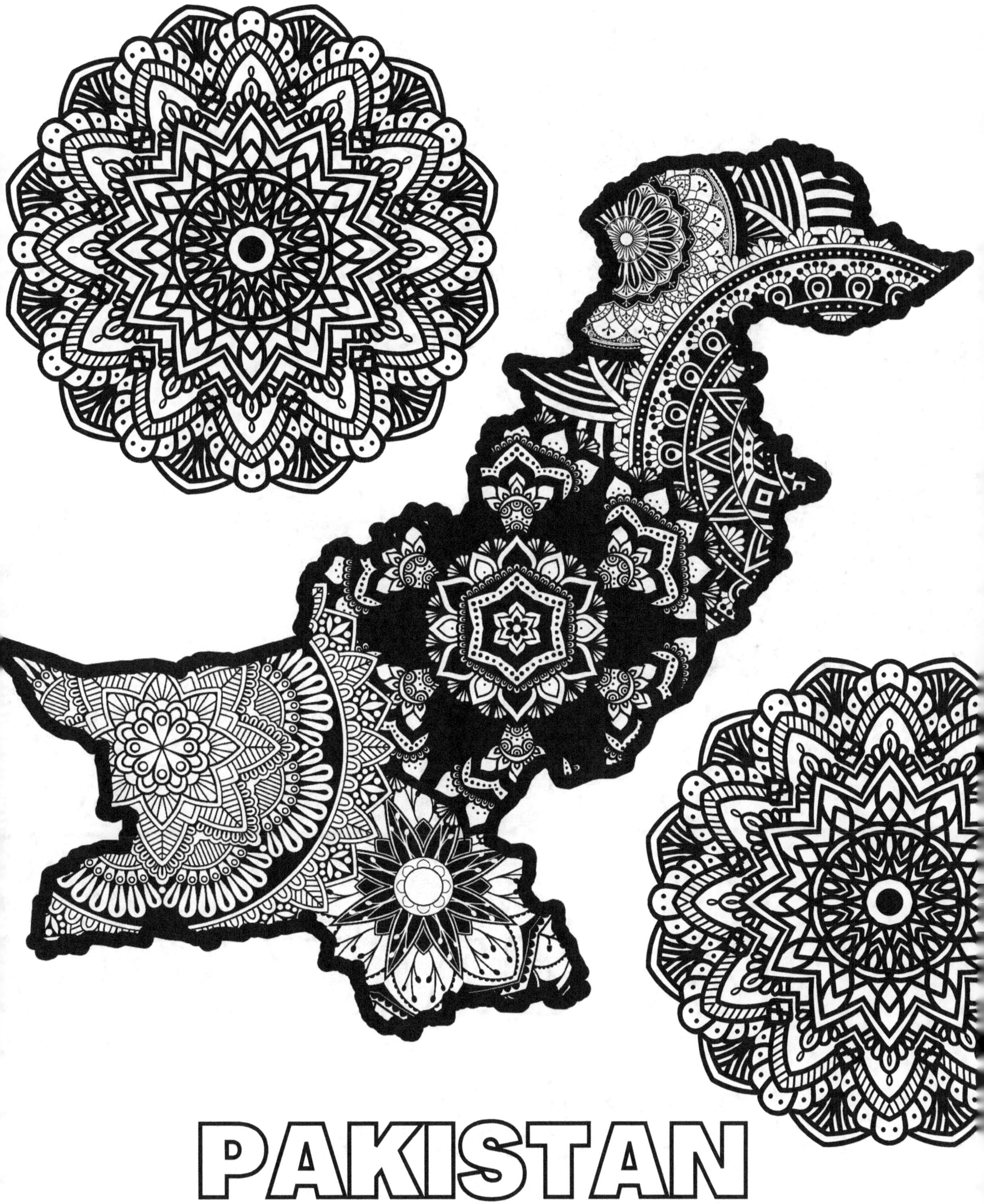

PAKISTAN

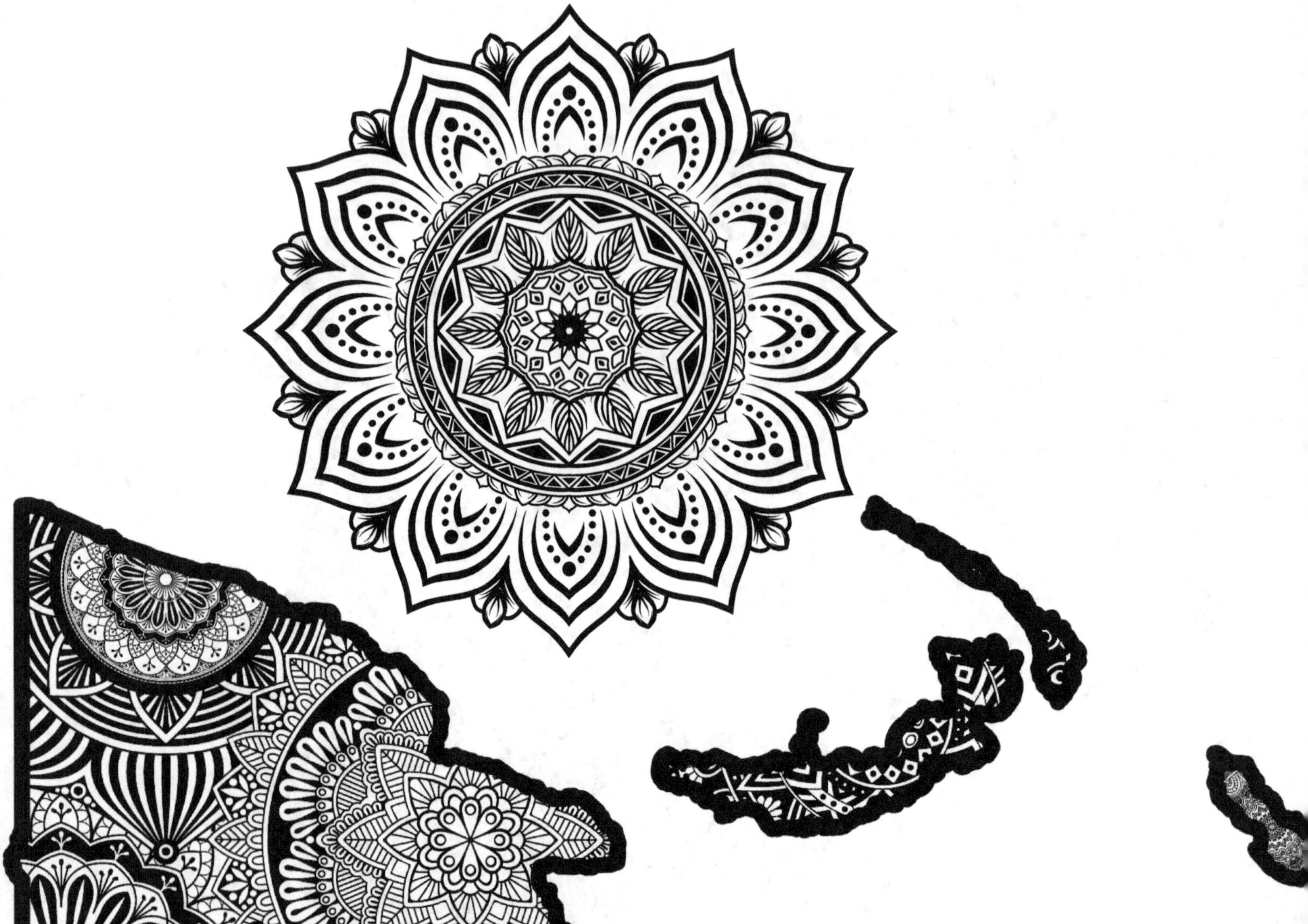

PAPUA NEW GUINEA

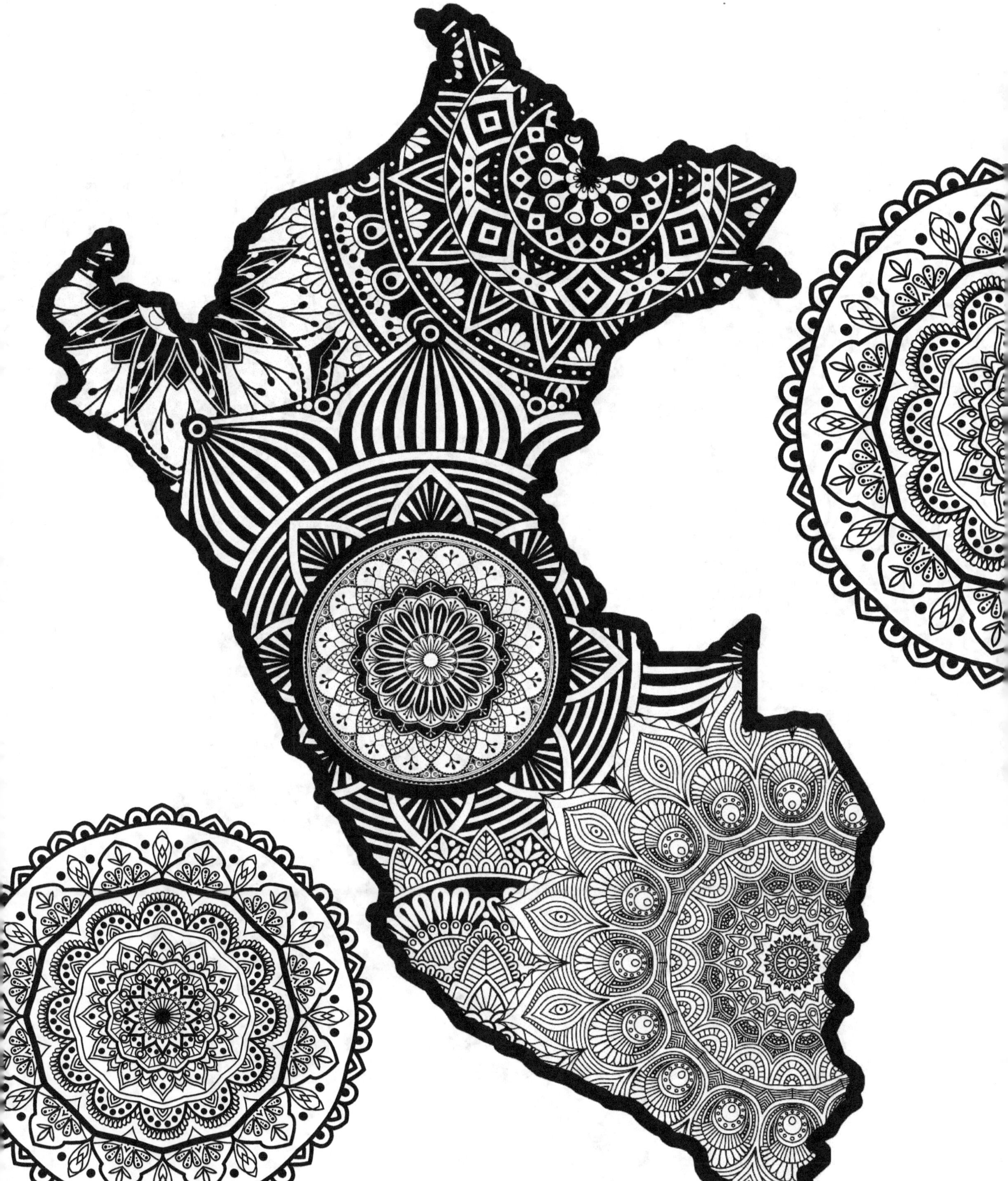

PERU

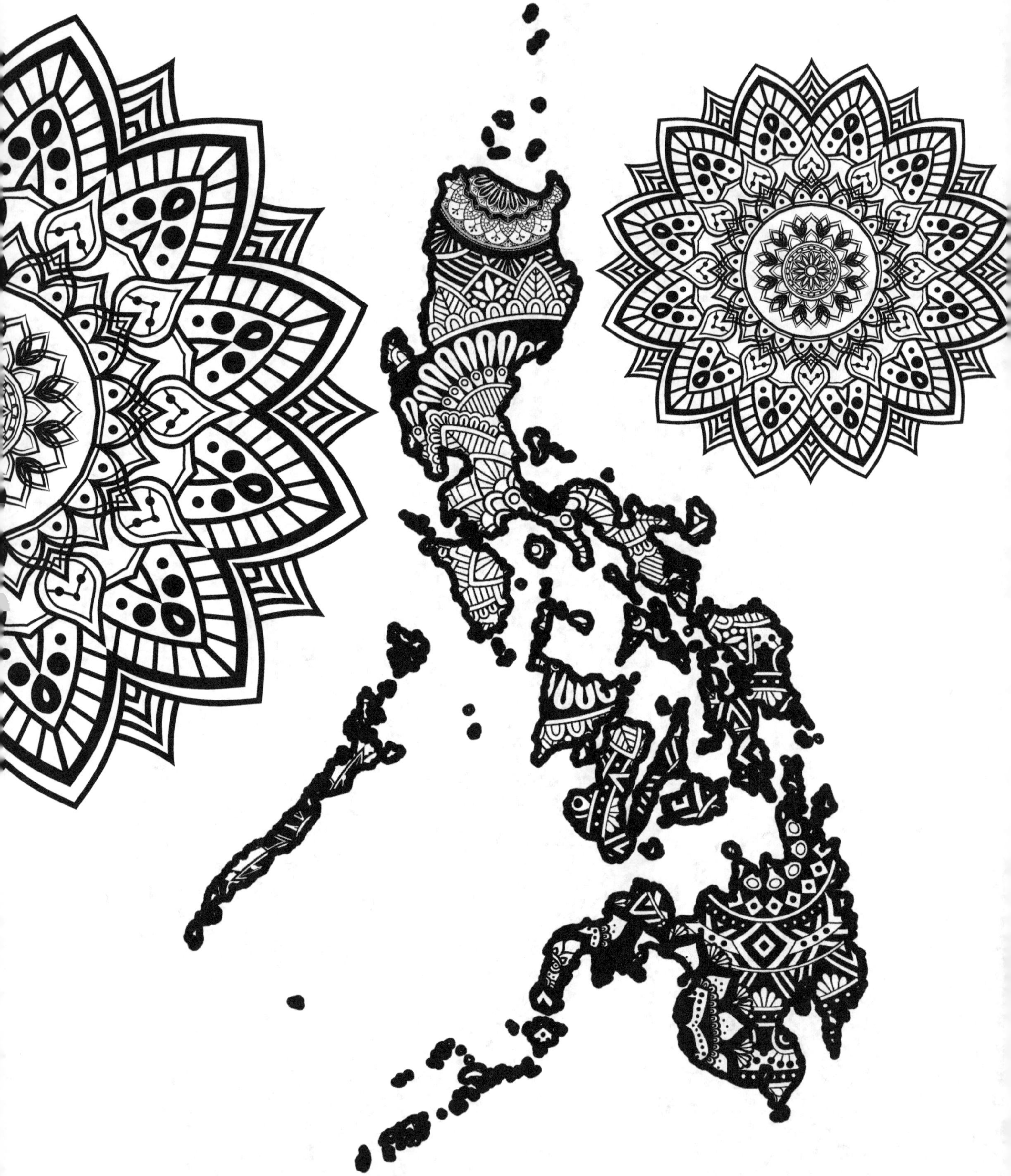

PHILIPPINES

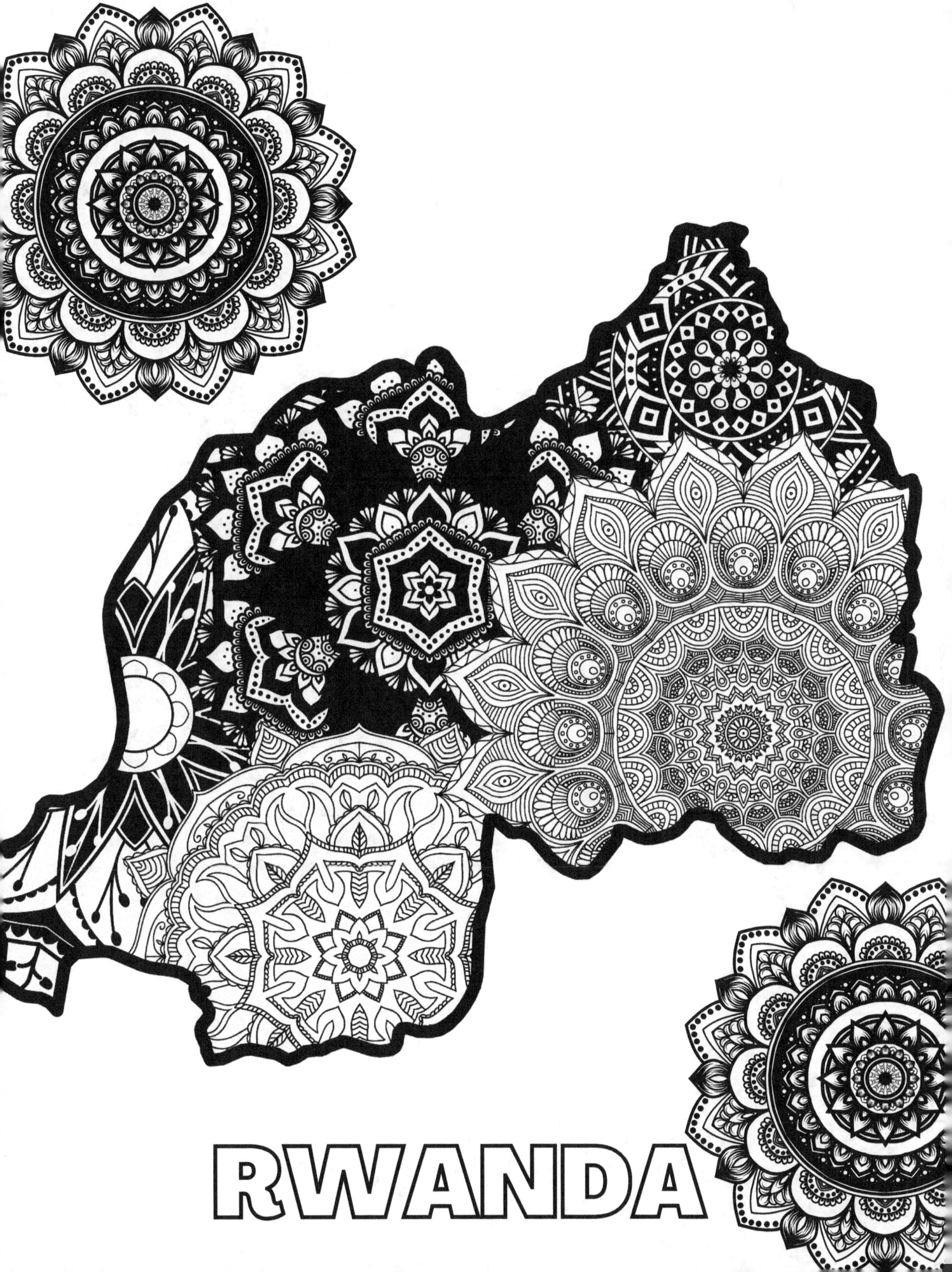
RWANDA

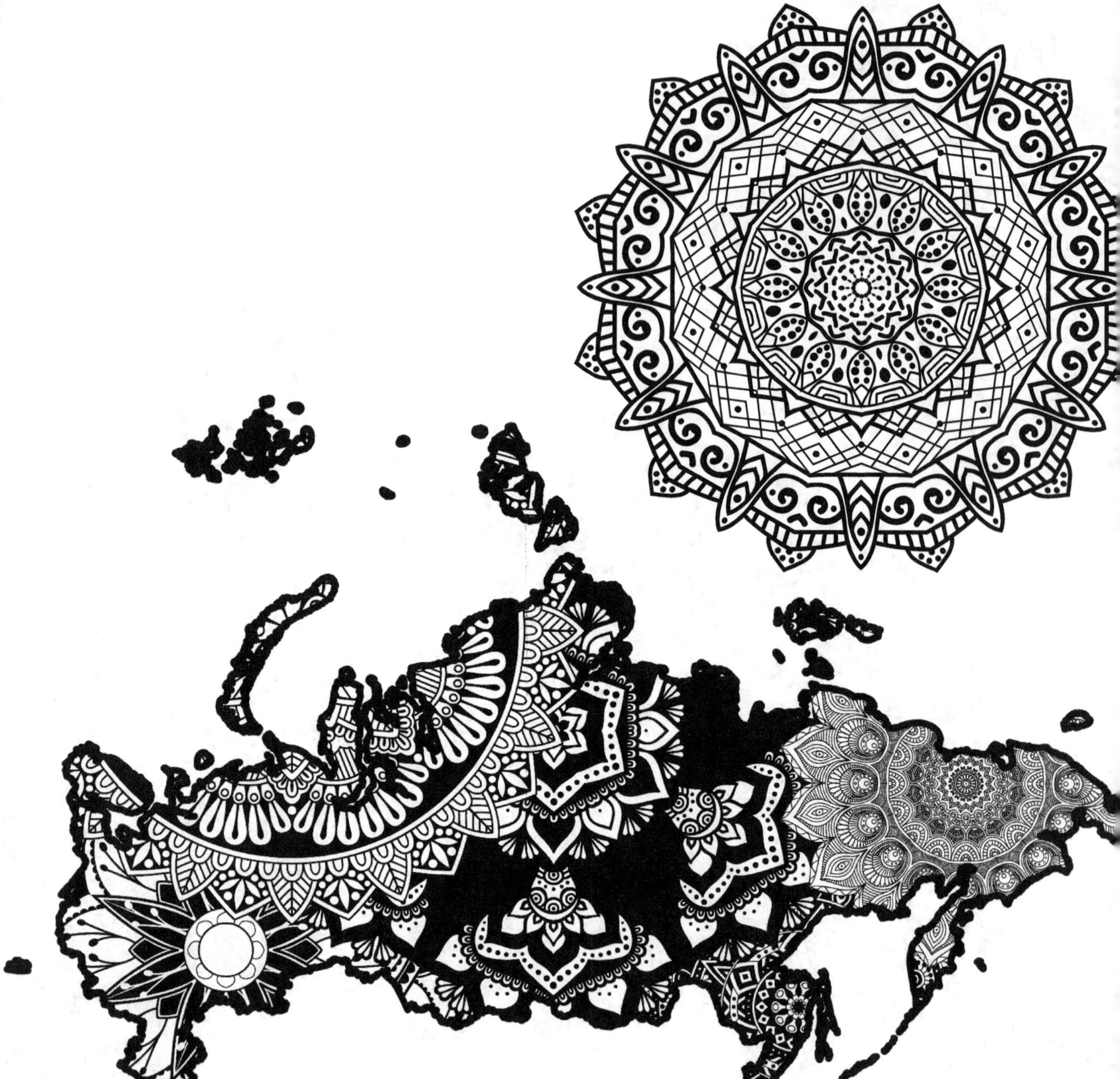

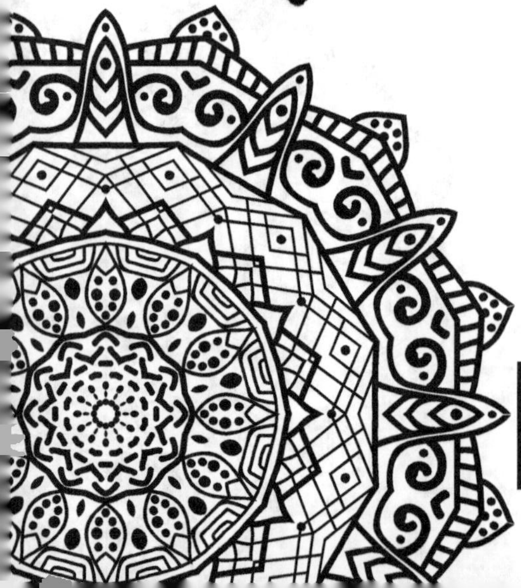

RUSSIA

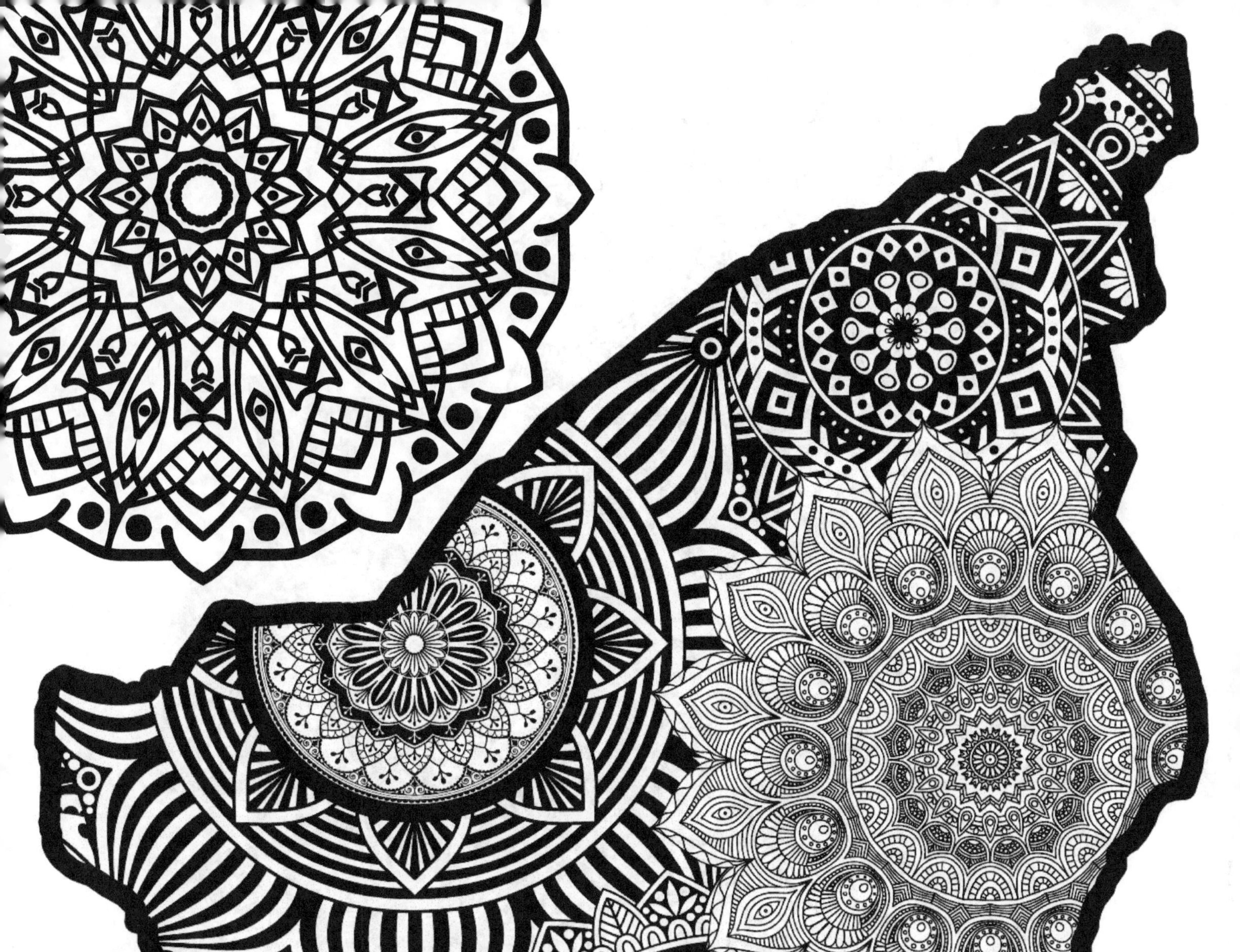

SAN MARINO

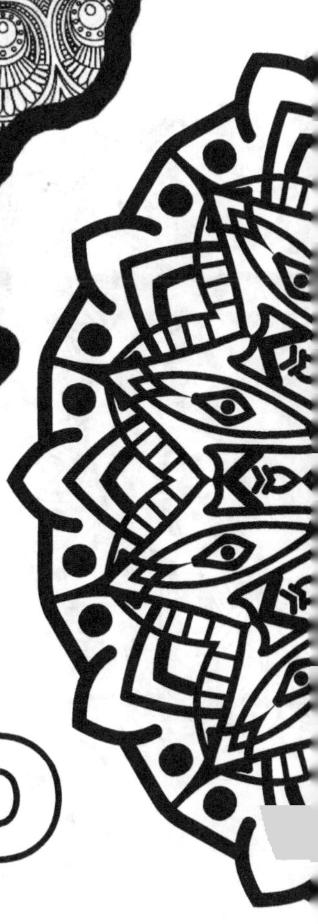

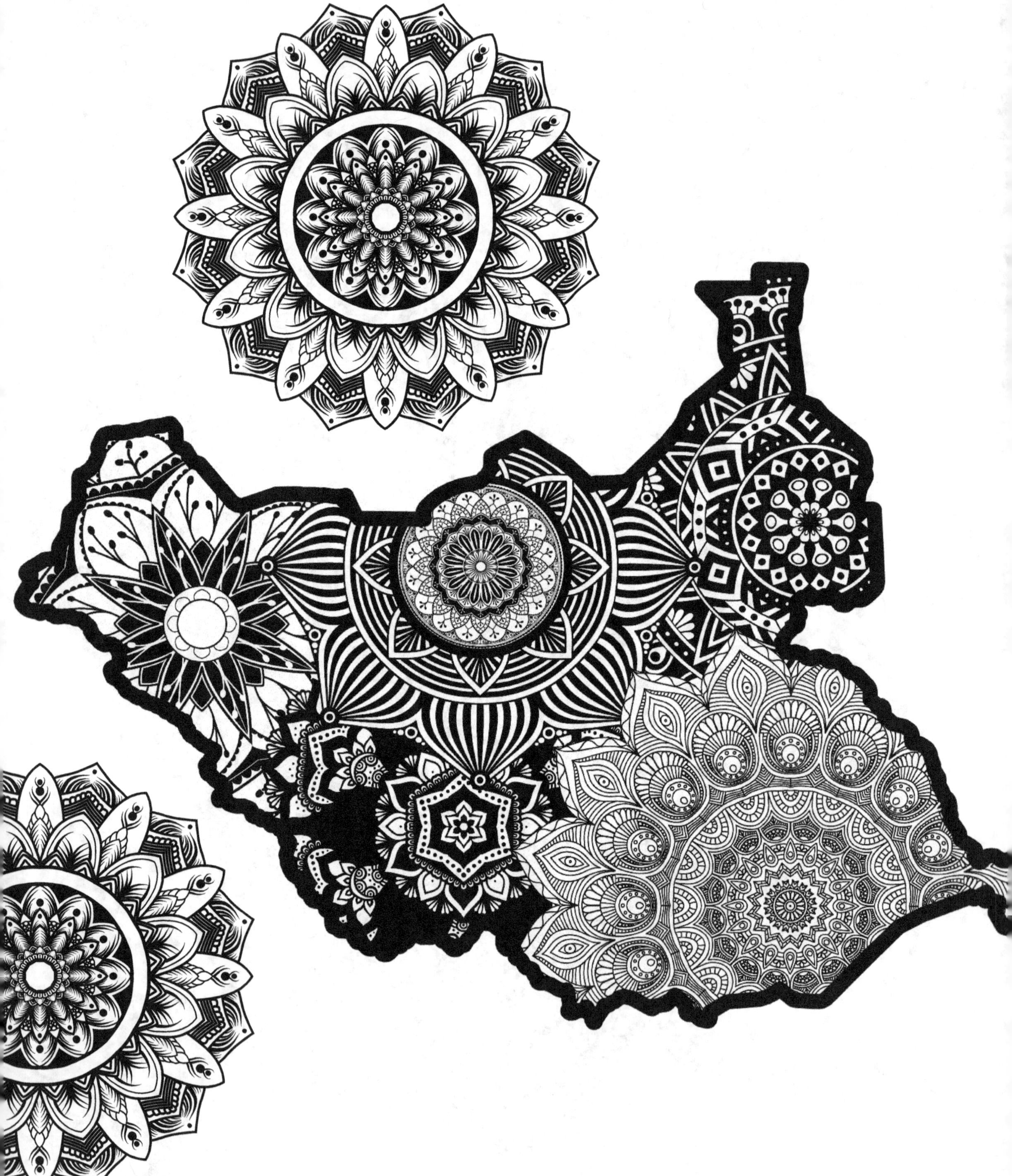

SOUTH SUDAN

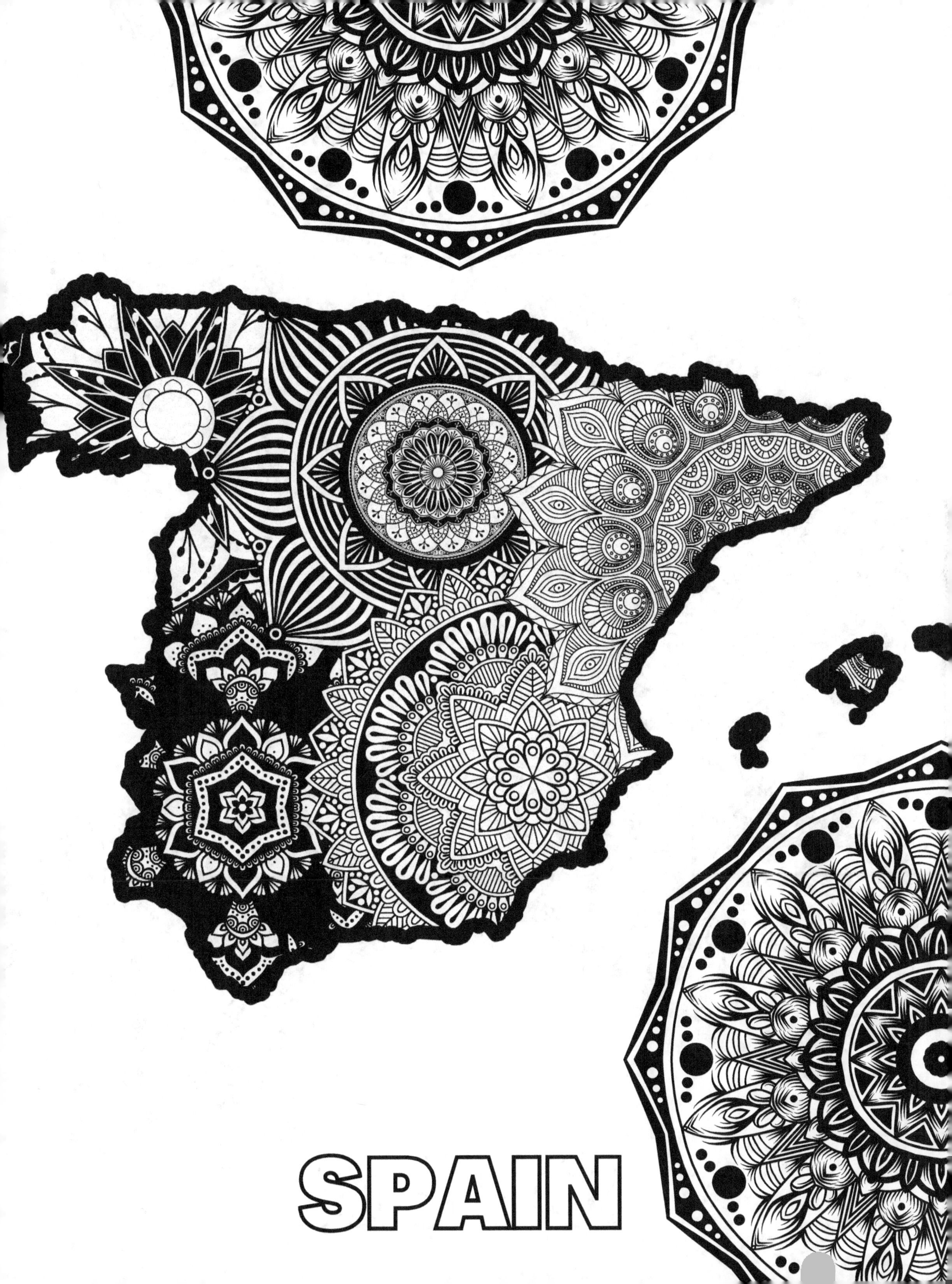

SPAIN

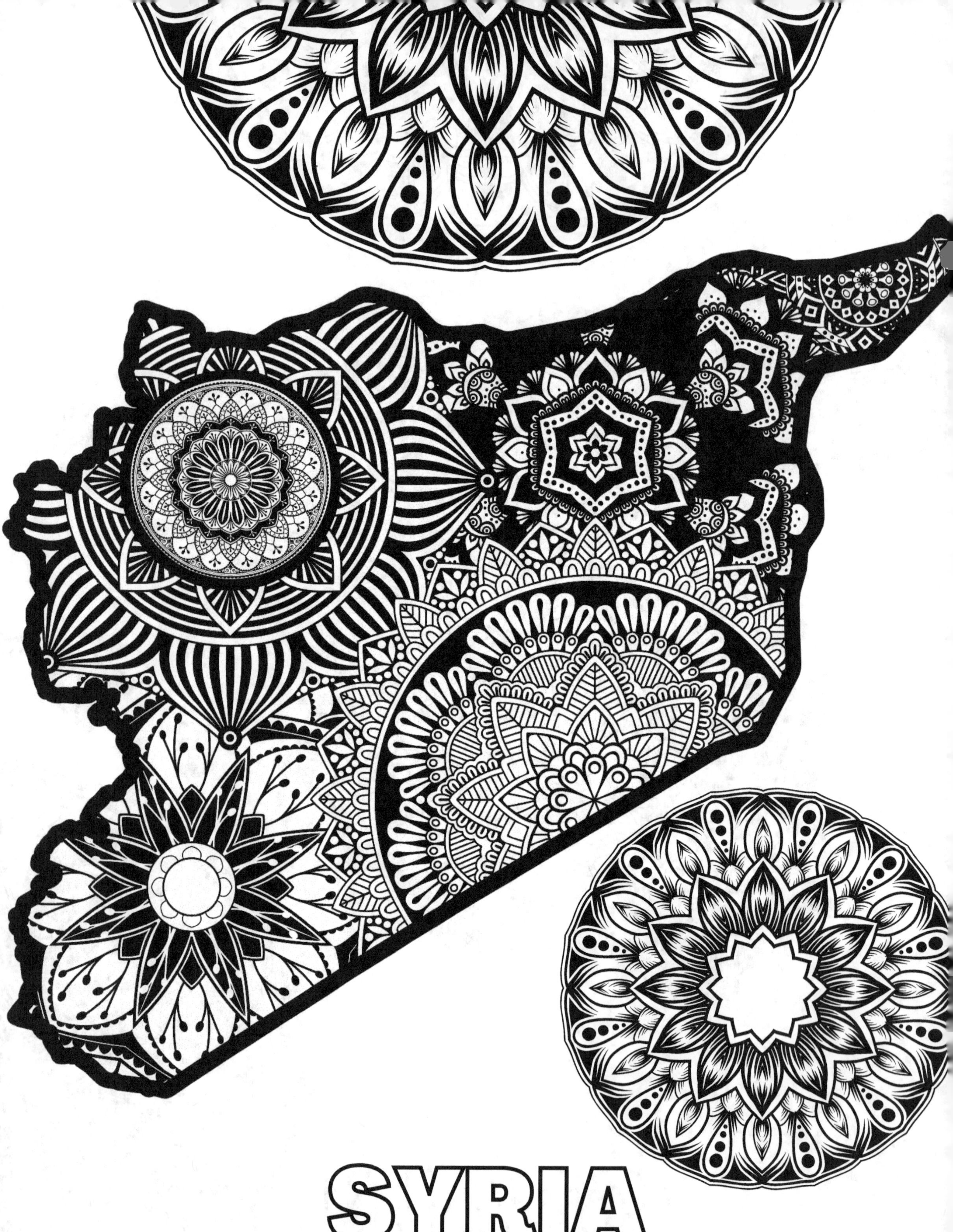

SYRIA

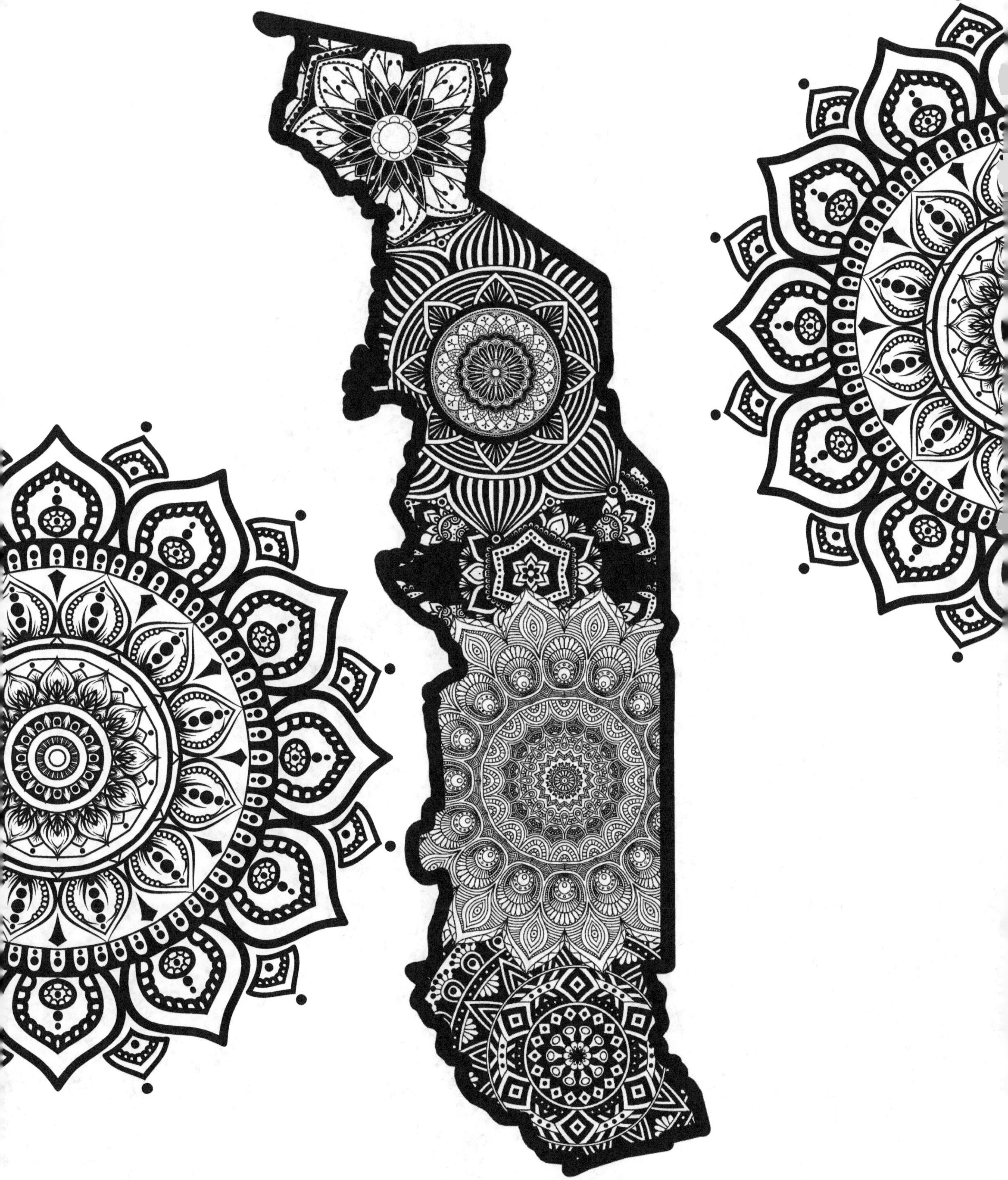

TOGO

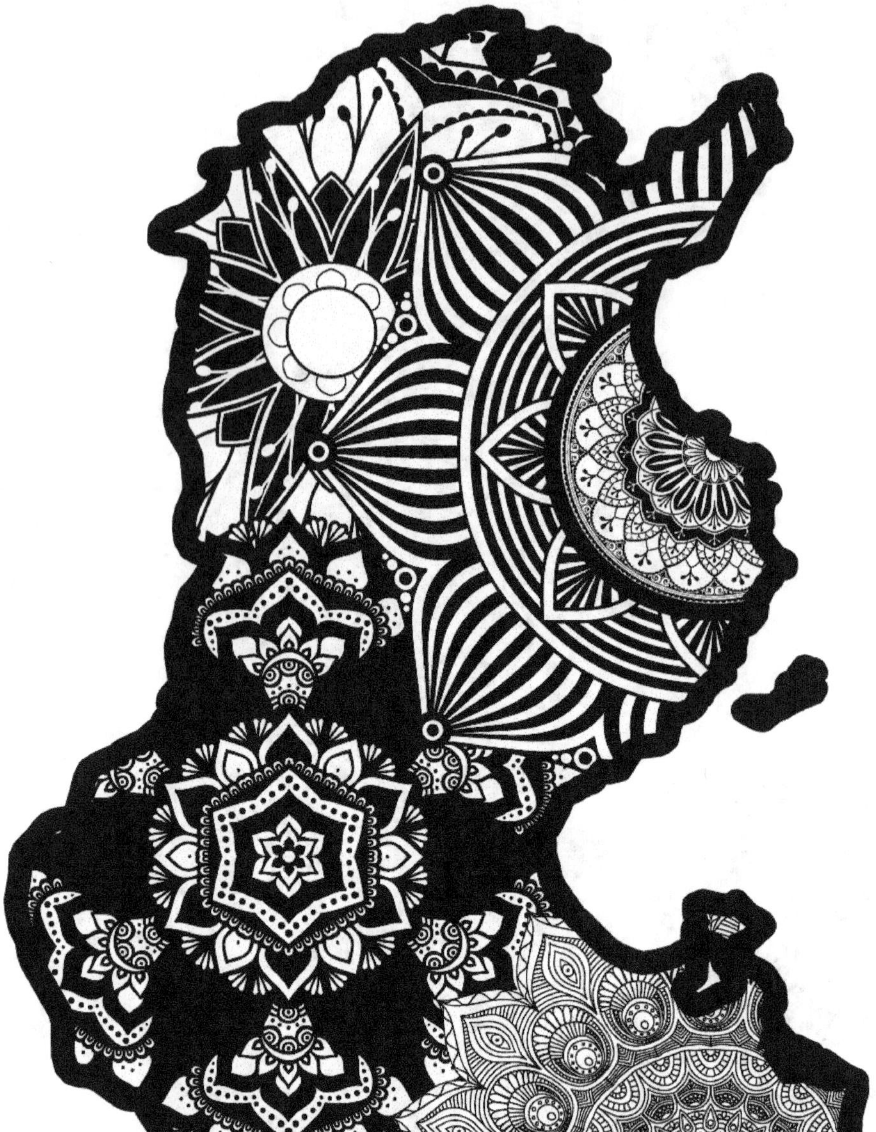

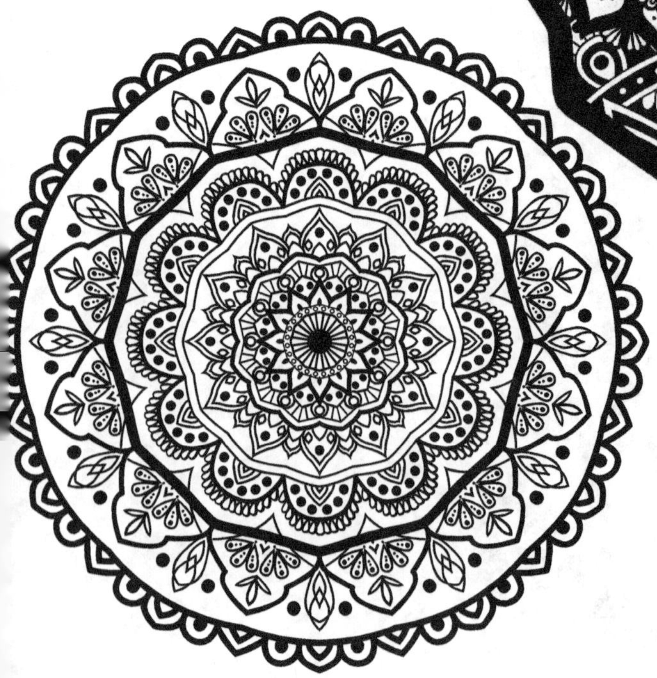

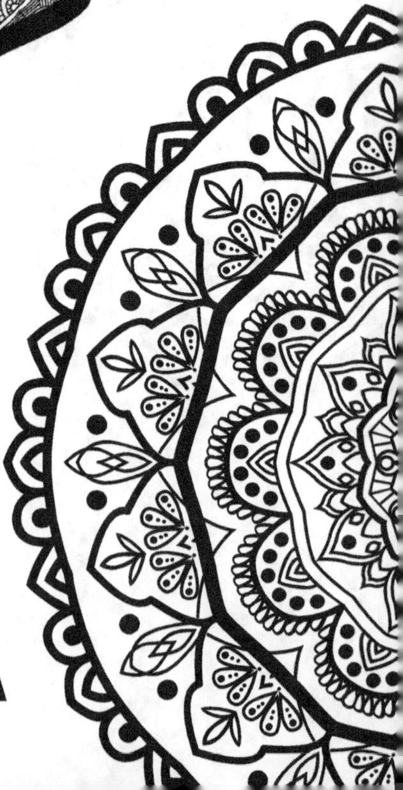

TUNISIA

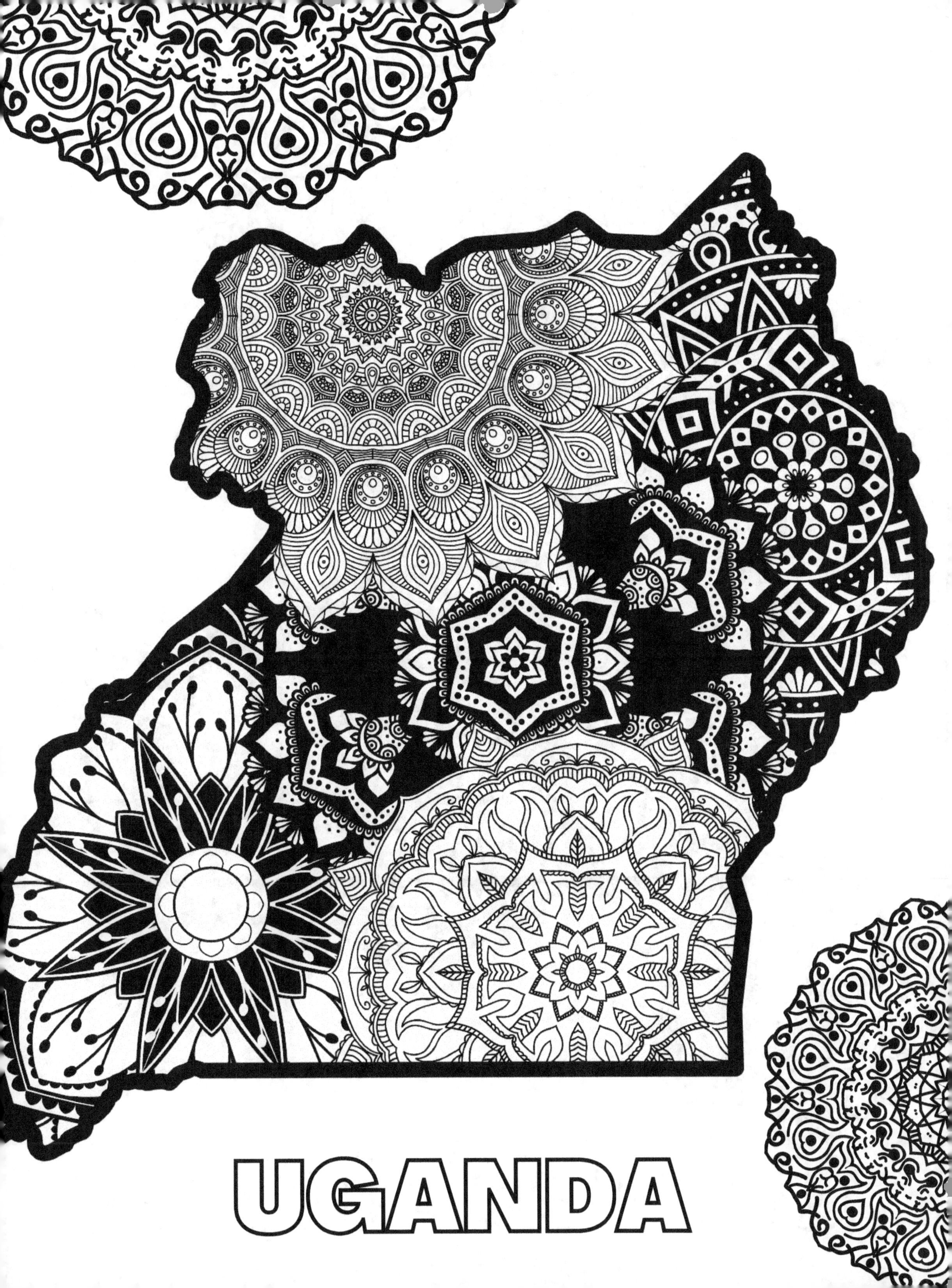

UGANDA

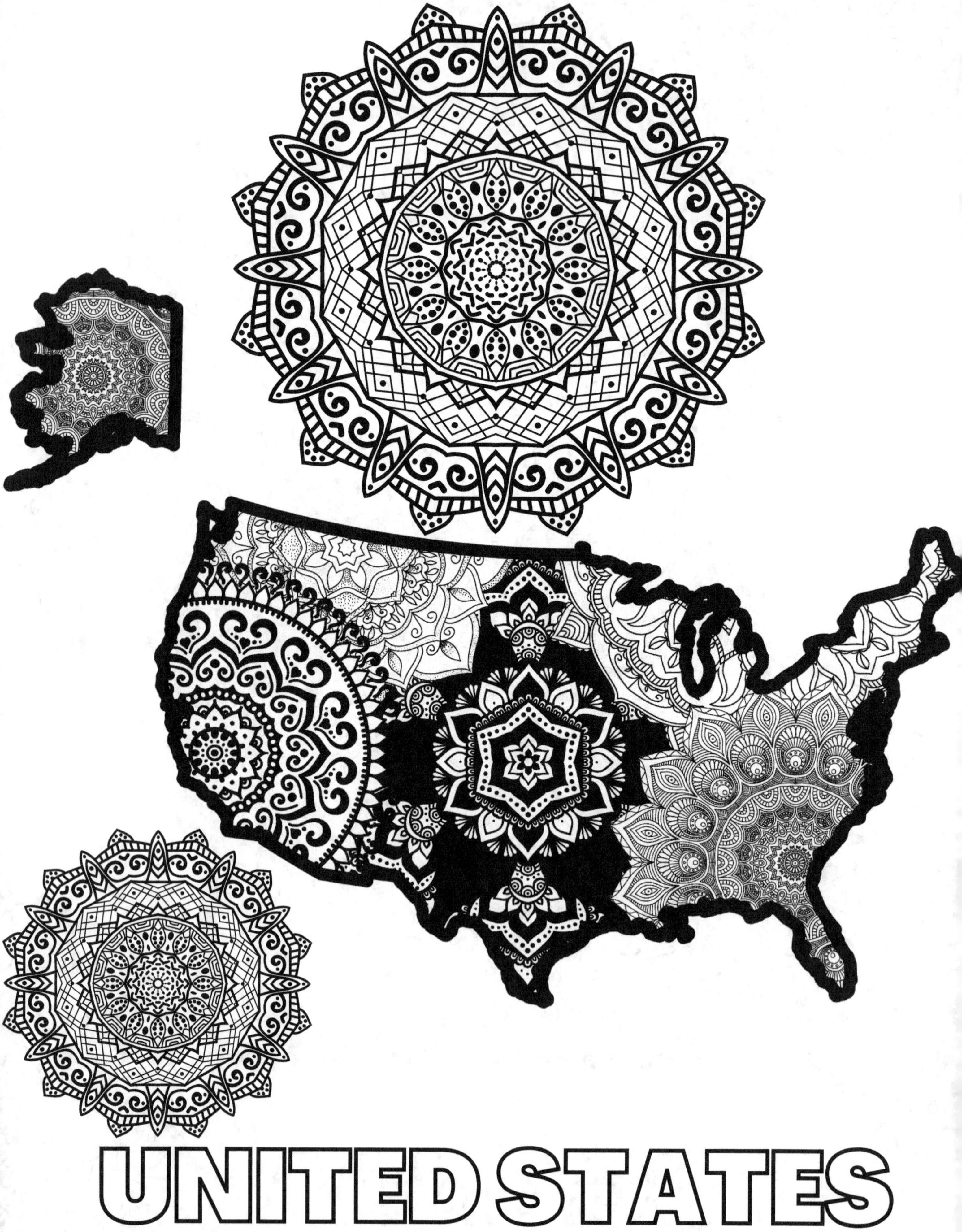

UNITED STATES

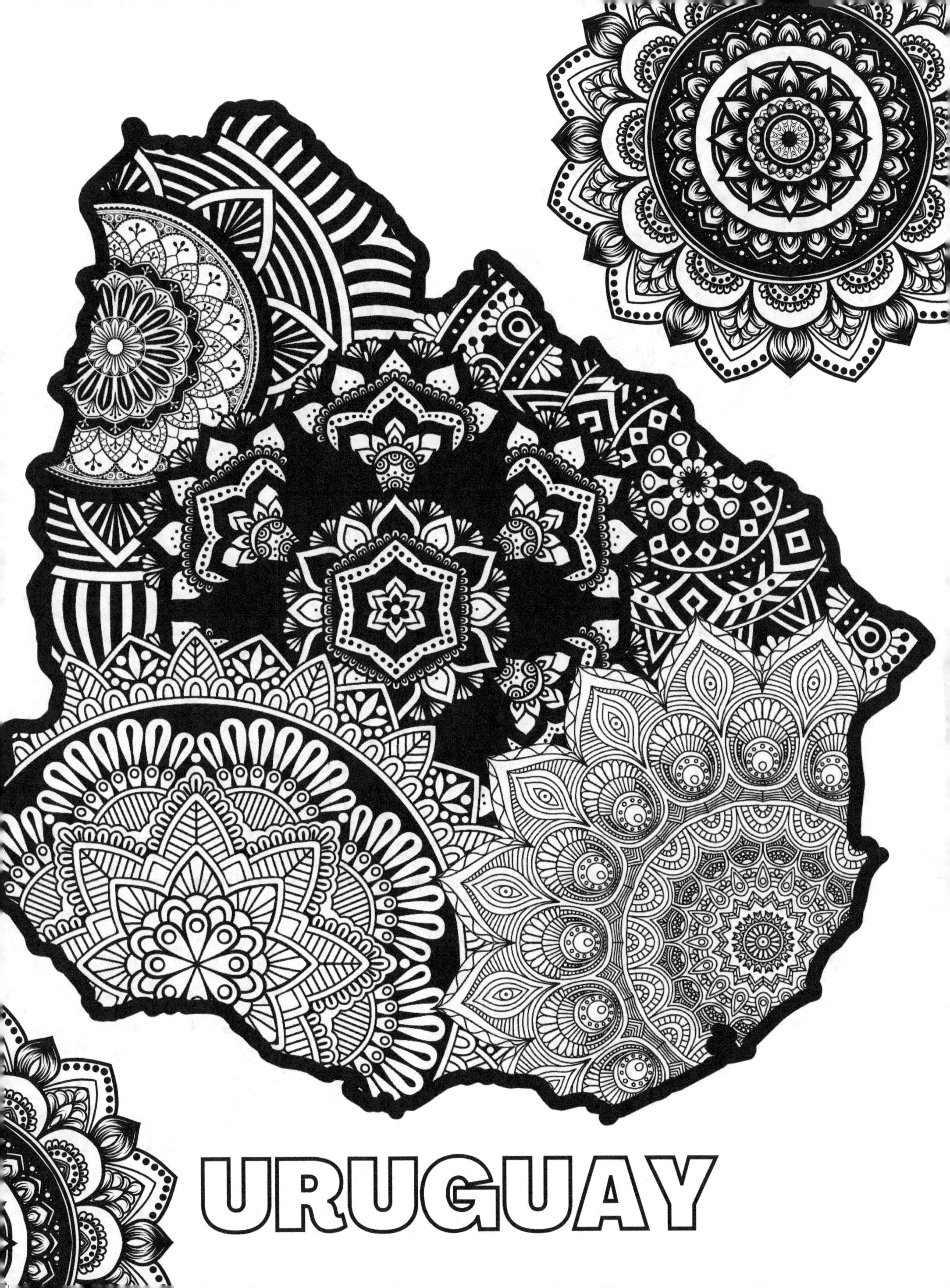
URUGUAY

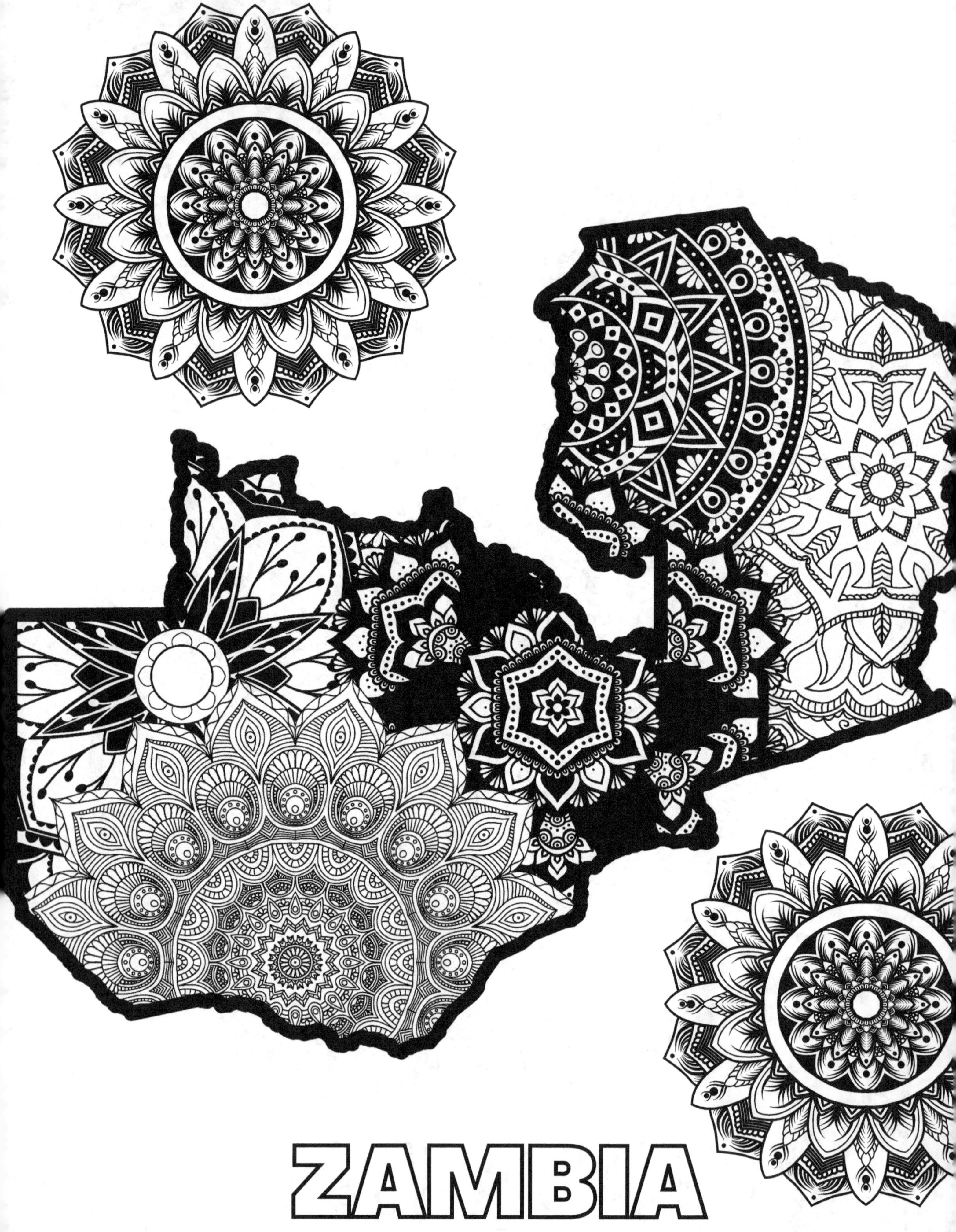

ZAMBIA

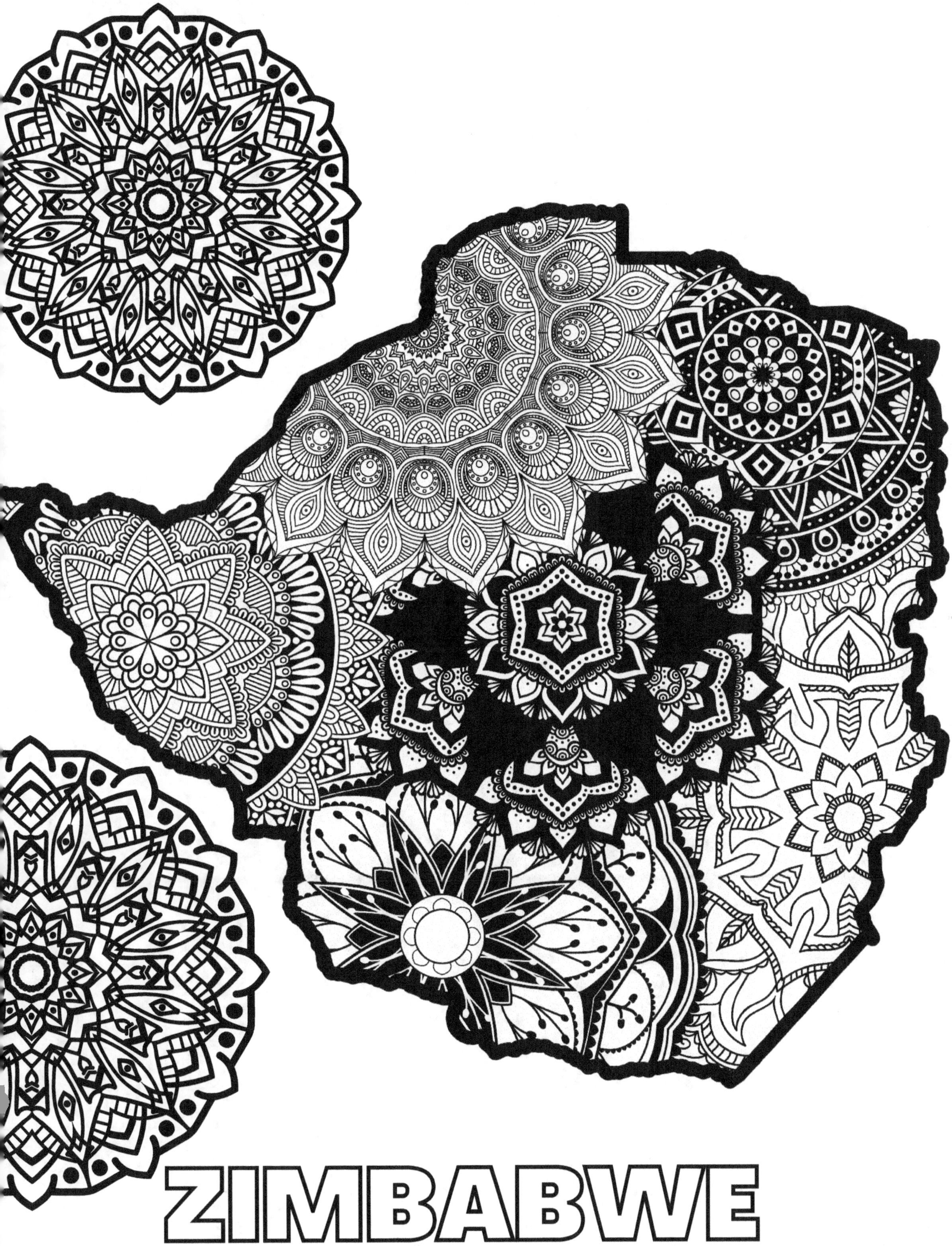

ZIMBABWE

www.ingramcontent.com/pod-product-compliance
Lightning Source LLC
Chambersburg PA
CBHW080955220526
45465CB00008BA/3295